Seeing Depression Through the Eye.
tive source of current biblical thinking abou
It is also an insightful and practical workb
homework with the depressed counselee. As June Ganselle .. _
us the heart-issues related to depression, we gain understanding in
to what motivates our thoughts, beliefs, and desires in our idolatrous hearts. She then offers us the "cure" – the gospel and Truth
from God's Word. I am excited to utilize this book as I counsel depressed women and teens because it offers a concise biblical way to
approach the struggle.

Ellen Castillo, Executive Director and Biblical Counselor, Word of
Hope Ministries

Having just received a new counselee struggling with depression, I could not wait to get into *Seeing Depression Through
The Eyes Of Grace*. Immediately I was able to gather homework
ideas, biblical truth and compassionate encouragement. I greatly appreciated counseling problems handled by topic. I was reminded of
Ephesians 4:15, teach the truth and do it with love and compassion.
Thank you for this excellent resource.

Patricia A. Miller AABC
Author: *Quick Scripture Reference for Counseling Women*
Biblical Counseling Program Chair
Calvary Bible College Kansas City, MO

Seeing Depression Through the Eyes of Grace

Julie Ganschow

Seeing Depression Through the Eyes of Grace

By Julie Ganschow
MABC, Certified Biblical Counselor

Published by Pure Water Press, © 2015

Cover design by Andrea Loy.

Unless otherwise noted, the Scripture quotations contained in this book are taken from the Holy Bible, New King James Version, © 1979, 1980, 1982 by Thomas Nelson, Inc., Nashville, Tennessee. Verses marked NLT are from the New Living Translation, © 1996. Used by permission of Tyndale House Publishers, Inc., Wheaton, Illinois, 60189. All rights reserved. Verses marked NIV are from the Holy Bible, New International Version, © 1972, 1978, 1984 by International Bible Society. Used by permission of Zondervan Publishing House. All rights reserved. Verses marked CCNT are from the Christian Counselors New Testament, Timeless Texts, Hackettstown, New Jersey, © 1979, 1980, 1994, 2000 by Jay E. Adams.

The Bible versions chosen for inclusion in this book are not intended as an endorsement of any particular version but rather for ease of reading. For in-depth study, the author recommends a more literal version, such as the New American Standard Bible or English Standard Version.

The clinical information presented in this book was gleaned from medical doctors, psychotherapists, psychologists, and psychiatrists. All "counselee" representations are fictitious and do not represent any one person living or dead or their actual case histories or personal stories.

Printed in the United States of America

ISBN-13:978-0692600504 (Pure Water Press)
ISBN-10:0692600507

Table of Contents

Foreword

This began as a little booklet I was putting together from notes I used in a FOCIS (Find Out Christ Is Sufffcient) group in 2004. I intended to use it with my counselees who struggle with depression. It has grown in both scope and volume and can no longer be considered a booklet.

I originally wrote this book because I was so concerned about the number of people I saw in my counseling center who were diagnosed with "clinical depression" or some form of it. Since that time my concern has grown as more and more people are being given psychiatric diagnoses for what appear to be very common problems like anger, worry, and anxiety. They come armed with their diagnosis, full of fear, and virtually without hope. The biblical counselor has a unique opportunity to minister to these poor souls, removing the shroud of hopelessness from the diagnosis and showing them answers from the Scriptures for overcoming depression. My prayer is that both biblical counselor and counselee alike will find this book helpful.

I am very grateful to my dear friend, Suzanne Holland, who has poured her heart and soul into editing this revision. The Lord brought you along at just the right time in my life, and I am richly blessed! Many thanks to my friend of many years, Jody Lokken. I am so thankful for your willingness to once again lay out this book for publication.

Last, but certainly not least, I thank my best friend and beloved husband. Larry, every woman should have a husband like you. You are incredible, selfless, and a steadfast example of quiet, great faith and trust in God. You are my always and forever love.

Above all, I am thankful to my God, Savior, and King, Jesus Christ. What you have done with this lump of clay is humbling and amazing to me.

How thankful I am to Christ Jesus our Lord for considering me trustworthy and appointing me to serve him, even though I used to scoff at the name of Christ.

But God had mercy on me because I did it in ignorance and unbelief. Oh, how kind and gracious the Lord was! He filled me completely with faith and the love of Christ Jesus. This is a true saying, and everyone should believe it: Christ Jesus came into the world to save sinners—and I was the worst of them all. But that is why God had mercy on me, so that Christ Jesus could use me as a prime example of his great patience with even the worst sinners. Then others will realize that they, too, can believe in him and receive eternal life. Glory and honor to God forever and ever. He is the eternal King, the unseen one who never dies; he alone is God. Amen.

(1 Timothy 1:12-17, NLT).

Introduction

This book is divided into two parts. Section One is dedicated to the spiritual and biblical aspects of depression. It is written to the one suffering from depression who desires to understand and follow God's principles for recovery. Throughout this section you will find boxes marked like this: ♥*Heart Work*. The questions in these boxes are intended to get you thinking about how to apply what you are reading. In a separate notebook or journal, answer these questions honestly and completely. While this requires effort and time, the benefit you derive from these exercises will be directly proportional to the effort you put into them.

Section Two contains updated medical and psychological thinking on depression, chemical imbalance, and medication to treat depression. This section examines the information from a biblical perspective and contains many references and quotations on the medical model, which will be useful for both counselor and counselee.

A Word About the Topic of Depression

With respect to the areas of depression and "mental illness," biblical counseling has received a rather negative reputation among certain medical professionals and even in some churches. A few think that biblical counselors label everything as sin, totally discount all organic brain illnesses, and want everyone off their medications. This is an unfortunate and false characterization of biblical counseling.

The responsibility of a biblical counselor is to help you in the process of heart change—to help you to understand the process of being transformed by the renewing of the mind through the Word of God.

Good biblical counselors will not have as their goal getting you off your medication; that issue is between you and your doctor. If you desire to discontinue your medication in conjunction with or upon conclusion of successful biblical counseling, you should be referred back to your doctor. Your counselor may be happy to work with your doctor in this matter, upon your request.

The medical profession and the "experts" tell us that depression is a biological illness, a sickness caused by a chemical imbalance in the brain. They classify depression as a mental illness. At this point in medical science, however, no one can honestly and definitively diagnose depression as a "mental illness" because there is no way to medically substantiate that claim.

No objective medical test exists that can prove a chemical imbalance causes depression, and even if such a test did exist, there is no way to determine whether the depression caused the chemical imbalance or the chemical imbalance caused the depression.

I encourage you not to blindly accept what anyone says on this topic. Please explore both sides of this issue for yourself. Your best weapon in this battle is information! You can find reliable information on this topic on the Internet and in print. (Section Two of this book cites numerous examples of the current medical and psychological thinking on depression, chemical imbalance, and medication to treat depression, but it also gives the biblical perspective).

My challenge to you is to look up these diagnoses in the Diagnostic and Statistical Manual of Mental Disorders-5 (DSM-V) published by the American Psychiatric Association. Research the recent articles and reports by psychologists who are now questioning the validity and necessity of the DSM. Look for clue words and phrases as you read about the causes for mental illnesses like "it is believed," "the theory is," and "in some cases." Do the same as you read the package inserts and the small print in the magazine ads for antidepressants and other psychiatric medications. Listen to how TV commercials for depression medications define a "chemical imbalance." After some research, you will be amazed at how little these experts really understand about the brain with regard to these theories.

Am I attempting to discredit the medical profession? Not at all. Medical professionals have the same desire as biblical counselors—to help people. You will find the biblical counselor's approach to be radically different, however. Medical professionals counsel people out of their psychology, while biblical counselors counsel out of their theology, which is based on the Word of God. Your thinking will be challenged as you go through this book. I want to help you see another viewpoint—a biblical viewpoint—on depression and its treatment.

Section One

The Spiritual and Biblical Aspects
of Depression

Chapter One
How Does Depression Feel?

We all may experience dark feelings of depression from time to time. They may come with the change of seasons from summer to fall and fall to winter, the birth of a new baby, the loss of a loved one, or the loss of a job. You may feel depressed because

of a relationship that has gone bad or a divorce. If you are a woman, you may feel depressed before, during, or after your monthly cycle. Sometimes depression seems to have no cause at all; which can be very frustrating to the person who is experiencing it and looking for answers and relief.

Personal Stories of Darkness

Ann's Story:

"I am just so weary and worn down. It seems that this feeling of overwhelming sorrow and anxiety will never change. I wake up with it, heart pounding, fearing another day and the next bad thing that will befall me."

Daphne's Story:

"I am numb. Life is a black dark hole from which I will never escape. I sit and stare, seeing nothing in my future. I dread the dawn. I feel sick. My stomach hurts, and I want to vomit. "

Heather's Story:

"No matter how hard I try, things never seem to change. I am so discouraged. I see no hope in anything. I know God is there, but He is silent. I know He hears me but has chosen to ignore me and my desperate pleadings. I just don't know if I can deal with this anymore. I have no real reason to feel this way and I just can't seem to get past it. I want to give up. I want to be out of my misery."

Phil's Story:

"My life has become a never-ending gray day. Certain times

are worse than others. When I wake up sweating at 2:30 a.m., and it seems that my brain is already running in high gear, I toss and turn, anguishing over being awake, knowing I will be tired and worn out before the day even begins. When morning comes—finally—the day drones on like a steady cold rain of fear, anxiety, guilt, sorrow, and regret. I welcome the night because it means the end of another miserable day, and fear it because I know I will only repeat the cycle again in a few hours."

Jada's Story:

"I see myself as a person carrying a large board on my back onto which large bricks are being thrown. Each brick is a problem in my life. Some sneak on, while others come crashing on me from outer space somewhere. The burden has become too much to bear. Even though I am on my knees under the weight of my problems, the bricks just keep coming. I am out of tears to cry. They do no good; tears change nothing. I am out of reason to hope. I find no joy in anything, even things that should make me happy only remind me that after this good thing, another brick will fall and steal my joy away again."

Robert's Story:

"Life is so hectic and out of control. I live life trying to please everyone and end up pleasing no one. I am ineffective at work and at home. My job is on the line because I just can't seem to get out of this rut. I can't concentrate, I can't think, I can't prioritize or make decisions. Life has become a dead end, and I see no hope of change."

♥ *Heart Work*
Your Story: Write out your own addition to this section.
Be honest and forthright with your thoughts.

Once while a friend and I were talking, we came to this conclusion: For each of us, the circumstance or situation that brings us to the point of depression or any other trouble in life is merely an instrument used by God to cause us to hunger—to come to the table of His grace and His healing Word. If you are suffering from feelings of depression, consider that you are being led to the banquet feast of God's Word, to the riches of His grace.

What Does the Bible Have to Say About Depression?

Although an explosion of depression seems to have hit our society in recent years, depression is not unique to any person or point in time. Look at these Old Testament exclamations of depression:

My God, my God! Why have you forsaken me? Why do you remain so distant? Why do you ignore my cries for help? Every day I call to you, my God, but you do not answer. Every night you hear my voice, but I find no relief.

Psalm 22:1-2 (NLT)

Turn to me and have mercy on me, for I am alone and in deep distress. My problems go from bad to worse. Oh, save me from them all!

Psalm 25:16-17 (NLT)

Listen to my pleading, O LORD. Be merciful and answer me! My heart has heard you say, "Come and talk with me." And my heart responds, "LORD, I am coming." Do not hide yourself from me. Do not reject your servant in anger. You have always been my helper. Don't leave me now; don't abandon me, O God of my salvation!"

Psalm 27:7-9 (NLT)

I think you will agree that the words of the Psalms are words of deep grief and sorrow. The psalmist (King David) clearly seems to be in a state of depression. He speaks of groaning, being desolate, affected, and crying. His words are so descriptive that you can al-most see him suffering. Perhaps you feel like that today.

♥ *Heart Work*
Write out some of the words that resonate with you from the Psalms above.

17

A depressed person may believe he or she is under God's wrath or being punished. Be assured that if you are a believer, God will never turn His face away from you, nor will He ever turn away from you in anger. You are a child of His by grace. God's pleasure rests on you because of Christ. Your feelings are not "punishment" by God for sin you committed in the past. I can say that confidently, knowing that because of Christ's work on the cross, we have been justified; we have been made right with God. His wrath has been propitiated, or satisfied. If you are not a born-again believer, be assured that there is hope and healing in Christ. As you read, you will learn how you can be sure that you have been made right with God.

How Does the Bible Define Depression?

You may be surprised to know that you won't find the word depression in your Strong's Concordance. The Bible uses terms such as *cast down, suffering, sorrow, hardship, trials, overwhelmed, burdens, troubled, dread, hopelessness, and tribulations.* The Bible teaches that these terms represent an attitude or state of mind of an individual who is focusing on real or imagined problems, diffculties, perils, or losses with an expectation of defeat and despair.

Definition: Depression is a debilitating mood, feeling, or attitude of hopelessness, which becomes a person's reason for not handling the most important issues of life.[1]

Not all sadness is depression. In spite of the world's catch-all label for life's problems, Biblical Counselor Debi Pryde says, "What the world labels as depression should not be confused with genuine grief and sorrow over real loss, temporary uncertainty in a crisis, biological disturbances that adversely affect one's emotions, temporary disappointment, or the understandable frailty in human beings that causes them to feel a sense of hopelessness not warranted by the actual facts when faced with physical fatigue or facing real diffculties."[2]

You may have any or all of those feelings when you are depressed, and your feelings are real! If you are struggling with

---

[1]Pryde, Debi "Depression" seminar notes from lecture at counseling conference in Lake Orion, MI, Oct 14-16, 2002
[2]Ibid

depression today, I am not going to discount your feelings and emotions. I am not going to tell you that what you feel is not real. You may feel sad. You may feel tired. You may feel hopeless and think all is lost. The truth is, hope is not lost!

I have told you all this so that you may have peace in me. Here on earth you will have many trials and sorrows. But take heart, because I have overcome the world.

John 16:33 (NLT)

The world includes your sorrows and despair.

God blesses you who weep now, for the time will come when you will laugh with joy.

Luke 6:21 (NLT)

Let's take a look at some important facts about depression. Depression has two well-defined features. Here's the first one:

Depression is Strongly Oriented in Feelings and Emotions

When a person experiences feelings of depression in response to a circumstance or situation, it could be called reactive depression.

Here is something that might surprise you: Depression is not an emotional problem. The emotions of depressed people are working just fine. Their feelings are functioning well! They feel sad, alone, tired, and despondent, like crying and sleeping all the time.

Almost everyone feels sorrowful, overwhelmed, or hopeless from time to time. However, it is possible your feelings and emotions may be working in complete conflict with the truth. In this case, your emotions are reacting to circumstances as though they are bad when, in reality, they are not. You may feel you have a reason to sorrow when none exists. It is your response to your depressive feelings that will determine the outcome.

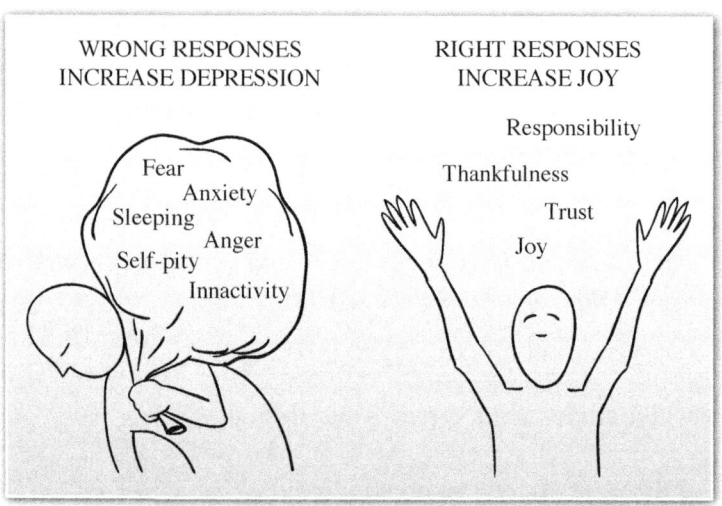

WRONG RESPONSES
INCREASE DEPRESSION

RIGHT RESPONSES
INCREASE JOY

Fear
Anxiety
Sleeping
Anger
Self-pity
Innactivity

Responsibility
Thankfulness
Trust
Joy

The second aspect of depression that distinguishes the biblical view from the secular is the connection between feelings and action.

How You Feel Becomes the Reason or the Excuse for Your Actions

People who struggle with feelings of depression tend to be very focused on their feelings. How they feel in any given situation dictates their actions. Many times, their feelings are out of sync with biblical truth.

Is your speech full of the phrase, "I feel?" I regularly challenge my counselees to pay close attention to the number of times the phrases, "I feel" or "I just feel/felt" come out of their mouths in conversation. Most are very surprised at the frequency of repetition. I challenge you to keep track of how many times in a regular day you hear yourself using the phrase, "I feel" in normal conversation. I bet you will be surprised!

♥ *Heart Work*
Do you make decisions based on your feelings?
How often have you done (or not done) something based on how you feel?

In the counseling room, the number of people who have abandoned thought and reason for feeling-oriented living often astonishes me.

Much like the humanistic psychologist Carl Rogers envisioned, we have become a society where it is acceptable and even encouraged to live life by how we feel. As a result, hearing a person express a thought or belief is rare. Listen to how others talk, and you will begin to notice how much people feel everything, even things that are not by definition feelings ("I feel like I should get a raise").

To express a thought or belief is to open yourself up for criticism or disagreement. Everyone is now "entitled" to express and live by their feelings, and it is rare to hear someone criticize another for doing so.

Do you think it is biblical to live life by how you feel?

Because Jesus Christ is our example, we must go to the Scriptures and determine if He lived His life by His feelings. A careful student will determine that Christ never commanded or suggested that we should live life by our feelings. In fact, the Bible warns us not to live by our emotions. First and Second Peter contain a heavy concentration of verses that warn against and give the result of living a feeling-oriented life. I have listed a few of them here for you.

As children who are under obedience, don't shape your lives by the desires that you used to follow in your ignorance.
1 Peter 1:14 (CCNT)

As a result, it is now possible to live the remainder of your time in the flesh no longer following human desires, but following God's will.
1 Peter 4:2 (CCNT)

Since His divine power has given us everything for life and godliness through the full knowledge of the one Who called us by His own glory and might (through which He has given to us valuable, indeed, the greatest promises of all, in order that through these you might have become partakers of a divine nature, having escaped from the corruption that is in the world because of desire).

2 Peter 1:4 (CCNT)

Especially those who are following the polluted desire of the flesh and despise ruling authority.

2 Peter 2:10 (CCNT)

Through uttering impressive-sounding clap-trap, by an appeal to fleshly desires and to impure practices, they bait a trap for persons who have barely escaped from those who live in error.

2 Peter 2:18 (CCNT)

Dear friends, as resident aliens and refugees, I urge you to keep at a safe distance from the fleshly desires that are poised against your soul like an expeditionary force.

1 Peter 2:11 (CCNT)

First Peter 2:11 is a personal favorite of mine in combating the desire to live in my feelings. The picture it brings to mind is one of being on safari where the hunter is often unaware of being watched and hunted by the prey he seeks to kill. Make no mistake, your fleshly desires will rule you if given the opportunity to do so. Feelings are powerful and can be very deceptive, especially in a person who struggles with depression.

Not only does the Bible reveal people who struggled with depression, but also it graciously teaches us how to respond to the feelings of depression. Here are several verses for you that address the various feelings that often accompany depression:

Anxiety
Cast all your anxiety on him because he cares for you.

1 Peter 5:7 (NIV)

Worry
Don't worry about anything; instead, pray about everything. Tell God what you need, and thank him for all he has done.

Philippians 4:6 (NLT)

Guilt

Let us draw near to God with a sincere heart in full assurance of faith, having our hearts sprinkled to cleanse us from a guilty conscience and having our bodies washed with pure water.

Hebrews 10:22 (NIV)

Sleepiness/laziness

Never be lacking in zeal, but keep your spiritual fervor, serving the Lord.

Romans 12:11 (NIV)

Sleeplessness

On my bed I remember you; I think of you through the watches of the night. Because you are my help, I sing in the shadow of your wings. My soul clings to you; your right hand upholds me.

Psalm 63:6-8 (NIV)

Anger

Don't sin by letting anger gain control over you.

Ephesians 4:26a (NLT)

Attitude

Be made new in the attitude of your minds.

Ephesians 4:23 (NIV)

Complaining/discontent

Do everything without complaining or arguing.

Philippians 2:14 (NIV)

I have learned to be content whatever the circumstances.

Philippians 4:11 (NIV)

Explosive anger/wrath

Your anger can never make things right in God's sight.

James 1:20 (NLT)

Frustrated, downcast

Why are you downcast, O my soul? Why so disturbed within me?

Put your hope in God, for I will yet praise him, my Savior and my God.

Psalm 43:5 (NIV)

Grief/sorrow, mourning

So with you: Now is your time of grief, but I will see you again and you will rejoice, and no one will take away your joy.

John 16:22 (NIV)

Godly sorrow brings repentance that leads to salvation and leaves no regret, but worldly sorrow brings death.

2 Corinthians 7:10 (NIV)

Grudge/refusal to forgive

Bear with each other and forgive whatever grievances you may have against one another. Forgive as the Lord forgave you.

Colossians 3:13 (NIV)

Overwhelmed, fainthearted

Now we exhort you, brethren, warn those who are unruly, comfort the fainthearted, uphold the weak, be patient with all.

1 Thessalonians 5:14 (NKJV)

Panic/fear, lack of trust in God

Such love has no fear because perfect love expels all fear. If we are afraid, it is for fear of judgment, and this shows that his love has not been perfected in us.

1 John 4:18 (NLT)

Self-pity, resentment, discontent, self-centered

But if you have bitter envy and self-seeking in your hearts, do not boast and lie against the truth.

James 3:14 (NASB)

For where envy and self-seeking exist, confusion and every evil thing are there.

James 3:16 (NKJV)

(Love) is not rude, it is not self-seeking, it is not easily angered, it keeps no record of wrongs.

1 Corinthians 13:5 (NIV)

24

<u>Self-willed, rebellious</u>

Some became fools through their rebellious ways and suffered affliction because of their iniquities. They loathed all food and drew near the gates of death.

Psalm 107:17-18 (NIV)

Scripture memorization is a very effective tool in combating feelings of depression. Select one (or more) of the verses above that you will commit to memory. Write them in your journal, and put them in your phone or other electronic device so you can recall them when needed.

Is Depression Different From Discouragement?

Some people wonder if there is a difference between being discouraged and being depressed. Discouragement is defined as:

1. The feeling of despair in the face of obstacles
2. The expression of opposition and disapproval.
3. To deprive of courage, hope, or confidence; dishearten; dispirit[3]

If you are discouraged, you may feel sad, weepy, troubled, or overwhelmed but still be functional. Discouragement is often circumstantial. Something you have put a lot of time and effort toward does not work out the way you wanted it to, and you become discouraged. When discouraged, you may fight through the feelings and do what is necessary in spite of how you feel. Sometimes discouragement is a catalyst to fight on and not give up. If discouragement were a color, it would be gray.

Depression is defined as:
The condition of being depressed.
The condition of feeling sad or despondent.
A reduction in physiological vigor or activity.[4]

---

[3] http://dictionary.reference.com/browse/discourage accessed 6/3/2013

4Dictionary.com, http://dictionary.reference.com/search?q=depression

Psychiatry defines it this way:

A condition of general emotional dejection and withdrawal; sadness greater and more prolonged than that warranted by any objective reason.[5]

Depression feels hopeless. Rather than leading a person to fight harder to accomplish a goal, feelings of depression tend to lead a person to simply stop trying. There is a sensation that things will not change for the better no matter how much effort or time is put into it. At their worst, feelings of depression can be immobilizing. If depression were a color is would be nearly or entirely black.

♥ *Heart Work*
Where are you on the scale of discouragement or depression?

Discouragment--Depression
I'm down but not out   I just can't anymore

Here are a few questions to help you clarify your thoughts:
- Are you presently immobilized by your feelings or circumstances?
- Are you so emotionally distraught that you feel paralyzed to the point that you are unable to function?
- Are you neglecting your responsibilities? If so, what are you neglecting?
- Are you trying to escape from your problems? If so, what methods of escape are you using?

Consider a young man named Sandy. A hard-working sales clerk in his mid-twenties, he works in a local sporting goods store and is well liked by his co-workers and managers. As the stores most aggressive, reliable sales clerk, Sandy has heard he is a sure winner for an upcoming promotion. When Sandy is passed up for that promotion, however, he becomes angry and depressed.

Over the next few days, his work performance begins to suffer and his attitude changes toward his job. After a week of this behavior, the boss takes Sandy aside and kindly lets him know the change has been noticeable. Sandy shrugs off this gentle rebuke and continues to decline in his work performance. He begins to skip work, staying in bed and thinking about how wrong it is that he

---

[5] Robert Smith, *The Christian Counselor's Medical Desk Reference* (Stanley, NC: Timeless Texts, 2000).

didn't get that well-deserved promotion. At work, he is sullen and cross with the other employees, and he bad-mouths the boss. When the manager confronts him with a verbal reprimand, Sandy begins to curse and blame the boss and other employees for his poor performance and attitude. He says he deserved the promotion but that the boss had it in for him. Sandy loses his job. He goes home and stays in bed for days, sleeping and moping. He ignores the phone, doesn't collect the mail, and doesn't acknowledge knocks on the door. After a week, his concerned parents come over and find him in bed, immobilized by depression.

♥Heart Work
Do you respond to those who attempt to help you by blaming them for your problems?

Do you justify your behavior, and demand that others change so you will feel better?

The Progress of Depression:

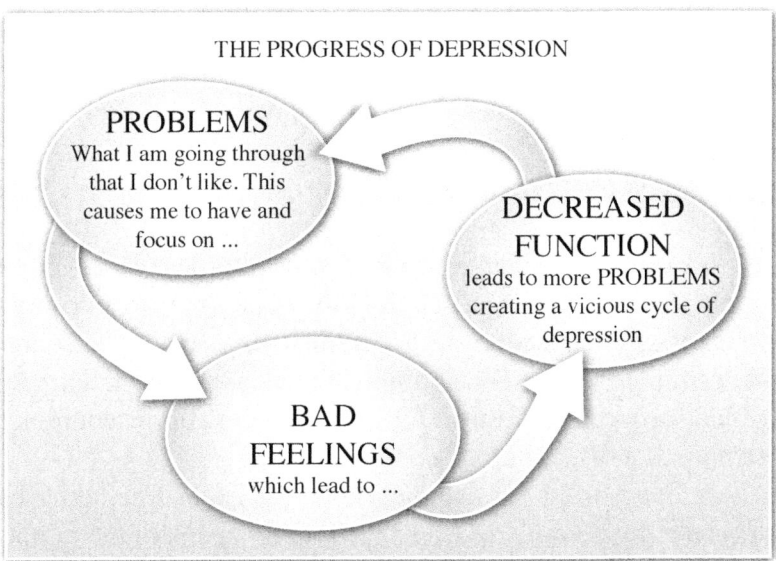

Those who are depressed describe the progress of depression this way: I have problems and I don't like what I am going through. This causes me to have and focus on bad feelings, which leads to decreased function, which leads to more problems, creating a vicious cycle of depression.

The Organic Causes of Depression
(Further addressed in Section Two)

Physical depression is the kind of depression that relates to or affects a body organ—it affects the physical body. Organic depression can result from a reaction to prescription medications, poor eating and sleeping habits, chronic fatigue, a sedentary lifestyle and lack of exercise, or too much caffeine.

There are presently more than 70 scientifically proven illnesses or diseases (organic causes) known to contribute to or cause depression, emotional disturbances, or bizarre behavior. This list of illnesses is not exhaustive but would include: Lyme's disease, hyperthyroidism, hypothyroidism, Cushing's disease, epilepsy, lupus (SLE), AIDS, diabetes, Alzheimer's disease, cancer, hepatitis, postpartum changes, and infections. Depression can also accompany organic brain disorder caused by a stroke, birth trauma, head trauma, brain tumor, overdose of drugs (particularly illegal drugs), or alcoholism.

Have you been diagnosed with any medical disorder? If so, is depression listed as a part of the disease or disorder?

Are you taking medication that lists depression as a side effect?

A careful medical exam is always in order whenever a person experiences prolonged feelings of depression to rule out any organic or physical cause for the feelings. A wise biblical counselor will encourage you to get a complete physical examination including blood work. It is critical, for the well-being of the counselee, to determine if a disease process is underway.

Have you had a complete medical exam (including blood work) recently? If not, make a list in your notebook of the symptoms you are experiencing, and the length of time you have been experiencing them. Use this list when you see your doctor.

If a physical problem is discovered, the elimination or medical management of the illness should be the first goal.

The biblical counselor's responsibility is to assist you in responding biblically to both the diagnosis and the treatment of the illness.

However, it is very important to note that in the majority of cases of depression, medical testing provides no objective evidence to prove that the body is functioning abnormally. In other words, there is no medical basis for the feelings of depression.

In *The Christian Counselor's Medical Desk Reference*, Dr. Robert Smith makes an important statement: "In order for something to be considered a true illness, science says that there must be objective, measurable, reproducible testing. To qualify as an illness there must be tissue damage ... demonstrated by abnormal function. It is a provable, knowable fact based on objective testing."[6]

This is important because despite a lack of medical evidence that a biological problem exists, many patients are offered medications to "treat" their depression.

Dr. Smith goes on to say, "The current method in diagnosing depression is based on subjective reasoning and thinking and not on changes in the body. Currently, there are no objective, measurable, reproducible tests for depression. Nothing exists to prove that it is provable or knowable as an illness for a fact, according to science."[7]

There are currently no tests that will produce definable and measurable data in diagnosing depression or any other "mental illness;" therefore, no basis exists to conclude that an organic illness is present in these cases.

Even if one day science is able to prove a causal link between genes and depression, will that remove the responsibility to respond biblically to something God has sovereignly allowed into your life?

Controversial Treatments

The lack of solid objective medical evidence for depression is the reason there is so much controversy in helping people who

---

[6]Smith, Robert, *The Christian Counselor's Medical Desk Reference* (Stanley, NC: Timeless Texts, 2000)

[7]Ibid

have feelings of depression. It is important for your overall well-being to consider this question: If it cannot be proven that a medical/biological issue exists, is it wise to apply a medical treatment? Some of the questions to ask are: Is it right to treat the feelings with medication and artificially cause the person to feel better? Is it better to avoid all medication use and only address the spiritual issues in depression?

We know that some people suffer to such a degree that they must have some help to get to a place of functionality, but that is not typical. Most of the time, doctors give prescriptions for anti-depressants because the patient complains of having bad or sad feelings.

Instead of trying to decide whether using antidepressant medication is right or wrong, a better question might be which course will offer the counselee hope and real solutions for their feelings of depression? In the case of a severely depressed person, it may be that short-term medication use will enable them to function as they receive biblical counseling that will address the root cause of the depressed feelings.

I believe that if there is no basis to prove a medical cause, a wise counselor will go forward with the understanding that the counselee does not have an organic or biological problem, but rather, a spiritual issue.

If you are depressed, your problem may not necessarily be the diffcult situation in which you find yourself. Rather, your problems may result from wrong or unbiblical responses to that situation. God has provided the means to live in the midst of the trial, but you must avail yourself of His grace.

Depression that is non-organic can be resolved by examining the key spiritual reasons in this book for why people experience sorrow without hope.

Spiritual Reasons for Depression

When looking at depression biblically, we must examine the root causes for the way we feel. With or without a medical diagnosis, the Bible directly addresses a critical component of depression.

Allow me to explain: Scripturally, we can safely determine that essentially we are comprised of two parts—material/organic/physical and immaterial/non-organic/spiritual. You have read that various diseases can cause or contribute to depression. If the problem does not originate in the physical (material/organic) part of the person, then it must originate in the spiritual (immaterial/non-organic) part of the person.

The root cause of depression that does not originate in the physical realm is found in what the Bible refers to as your heart.

Definition of the Heart

The heart is the biblical word used to describe the inner person. The heart is the immaterial (non-flesh) part of you that includes your thoughts, beliefs, desires, mind, feelings, intentions, emotions, soul, will, conscience and other aspects of you that we know exist, but cannot be touched.

Above all else, guard your heart, for it affects everything you do.
Proverbs 4:23 (NLT)

What you think, believe and desire in your immaterial part (mind, heart, soul, feelings, conscience, will, emotions) is what your material part (body) follows. You think a thought and your body responds accordingly. You may be so accustomed to your body automatically responding to these commands that you may not even think about them as you are doing them! We call these habits. We form many different habits by repeating tasks so often that we are able to perform them seemingly without conscious effort. Perhaps you can recall a time you pulled your car into the driveway but didn't actually recall driving home from work or the store. You were deep in thought yet out of habit your body performed the functions of operating the car flawlessly and bringing you safely to your destination because you have repeated that drive so many times before.

Many kinds of thoughts and desires may initiate an automatic or habitual response. When you feel angry, for example, you may scream and rant or you might quietly seethe. When you desire escape from problems, you may sleep, drink, or use drugs. When you are in trouble, you may lie to avoid exposure and discipline. These responses may have become automatic for you. Probably without your direct knowledge, you have trained yourself to react in a certain way when confronted by a circumstance or situation.

♥ *Heart Work*
What are some of the habitual responses you have established in your life? Make a list in your notebook of everything you can think of.

Whether you tend to scream, drink, lie, or do some other behavior, through repetition it has become a pattern of life. These sinful patterns are habits of the heart. The Bible has much to say about the heart as the vital spiritual organ in the body.

> *The good man brings good things out of the good stored up in his heart, and the evil man brings evil things out of the evil stored up in his heart. For out of the overflow of his heart his mouth speaks.*
>
> Luke 6:45 (NIV)

> *But the things that come out of the mouth come from the heart, and these make a man 'unclean.' For out of the heart come evil thoughts, murder, adultery, sexual immorality, theft, false testimony, slander.*
>
> Matthew 15:18-19 (NIV)

♥ *Heart Work*
Take a few moments and reflect on the verses above, then answer the following questions: What words and actions come from the overflow of your heart? Do you struggle with evil thoughts, bitterness, immorality, lying, or gossip?

We see how God views your heart in Jeremiah 17:9. I have one version of the verse below. Take a moment and look it up in other Bible versions such as the NIV, NASB, and ESV.

> *The heart is deceitful above all things, And desperately wicked; Who can know it?*
>
> Jeremiah 17:9 (NKJV)

The deceitful heart is bent on satisfying me, having my own way, and living life for my own pleasure, with me at the center of my universe.

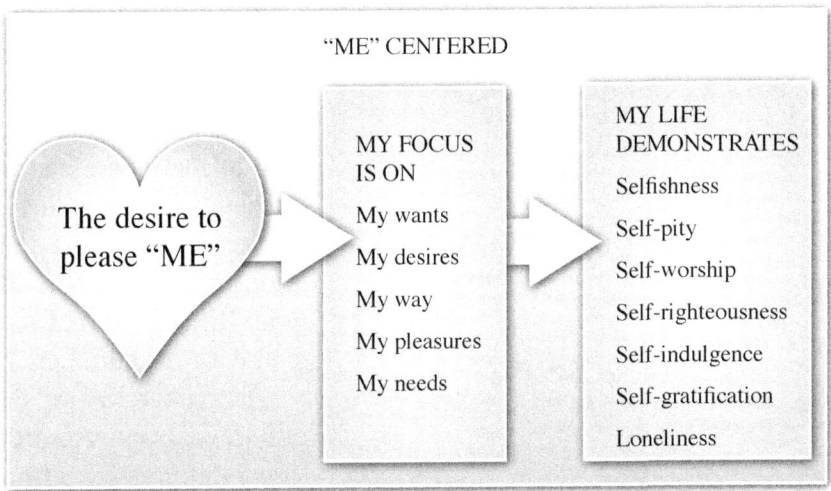

As you look at the above diagram, consider this: Because the heart can be referred to as the control center of your being, what you think, believe, and desire in your heart is what guides and determines your actions. If you are like most people, you do not naturally think about your heart being wicked. Perhaps your friends and family refer to you as having a good heart or a big heart. Maybe you have never before heard someone say that the heart is deceitful and desperately wicked. However, as you are working through this section, you may be realizing that you have some of the sin habits found in the verses I cited from Luke 6 and Matthew 15. Those sins are the results of sinful thoughts, beliefs, and desires. Here is something important to remember: Every action begins as a thought. The thought is fueled by a desire or belief. The desire or belief originates in the heart, and this is what leads to your actions. (For more insight into this subject, see my booklet, *The Process of Biblical Change*.[8]

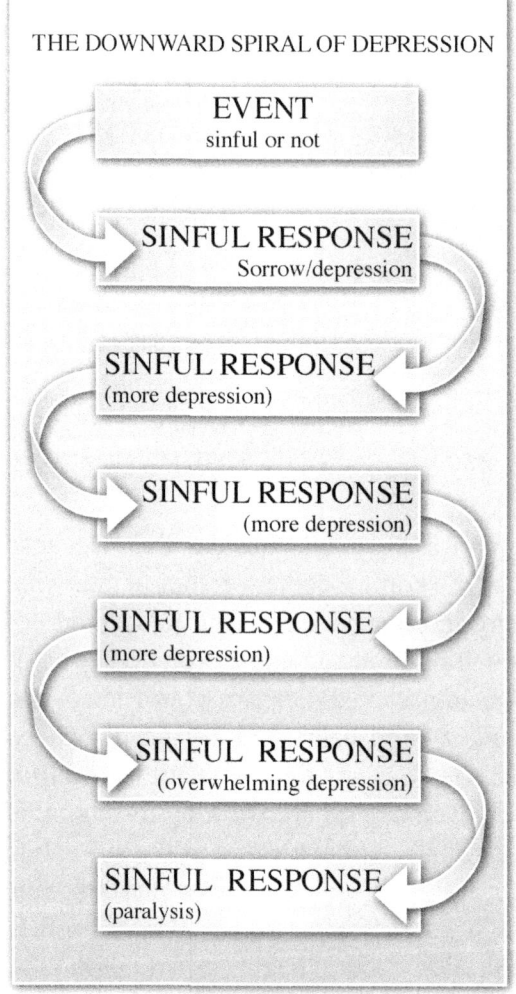

THE DOWNWARD SPIRAL OF DEPRESSION

EVENT
sinful or not

SINFUL RESPONSE
Sorrow/depression

SINFUL RESPONSE
(more depression)

SINFUL RESPONSE
(more depression)

SINFUL RESPONSE
(more depression)

SINFUL RESPONSE
(overwhelming depression)

SINFUL RESPONSE
(paralysis)

What you have been thinking about, believing, and desiring in your heart is what has caused you to feel depressed or to have sorrow without hope. God is using this time of depression in your life to reveal the contents of your heart.

The diagram to the left reveals how a person progresses from their original problem to being immobilized by feelings of depression. Regardless of the origin of the feelings, continued wrong responses to various situations and repeated wrong thinking produce more sin. There is always a choice in how to respond in every situation. The downward process can be halted at any point in the progres-

---

[8]Ganschow, Julie, *The Process of Biblical Change* (Kansas City, MO: Pure Water Press, 2009) Available on Amazon,

34

sion by correcting unbiblical thinking and replacing it with biblical thinking that honors and glorifies God and restores hope to the one who suffers.

Biblical Principles for Dealing With Depression and Sin

To deal biblically with depression, you must learn what God says about your problem. To start, God says that what you are thinking, believing, and desiring in your heart needs to be dominated by Him through His Word.

> *As the Word of God enters your mind and heart, you will begin to have a better idea of God's thoughts, standards, and goals for you. This is called being renewed in the spirit of your mind.*
>
> Ephesians 4:23 (NLT)

> *Do not conform any longer to the pattern of this world, but be transformed by the renewing of your mind. Then you will be able to test and approve what God's will is—his good, pleasing and perfect will.*
>
> Romans 12:2 (NIV)

A wise counselor will help you to understand what God has to say about your thoughts, desires, and affections of the heart, and will help you understand that all you do or say is a result of what you are thinking.

Examine Your Beliefs

Before you can change what you habitually do, you must change how you habitually think. You have to come to believe or think differently about depression in your mind because this will determine how you respond to it. If you believe depression is largely biological (genetic), or if the depression is a side-effect of another medical problem or head trauma, you may think the most you can do is get long-term therapy or take a pill to feel better.

Regardless of the etiology of depression, you are responsible to address it biblically. Ask the Lord's help in examining your heart regarding the thoughts, belief, and desires that lead to your behavior. You may come to see that regardless of the reason for the feelings of depression that your behavior is ungodly and that living a depressed way of life is unbiblical. This will require a shift in your core beliefs that will lead you to repentance.

Repent

It is important to note that repentance is a manifestation of the life of Christ within you. It is a proof of salvation in your life. The sinner is cut deeply to the heart by the Spirit of God and/or the Word of God and understands that his sin is grievous to the Lord. Because of accepting and understanding that spiritual reality, he no longer desires to participate in it.

Stopping the depressive behavior because of the consequences of your sinful behavior is not repentance. It is worldly sorrow or what John MacArthur calls "unsanctified remorse."[9] Its focus is on how the sin or its exposure will affect you.

Understand: Words Matter

Much of how we understand something depends on the language used to describe it. It is important that you understand the terminology being used to describe your behaviors and feelings. Also important is knowing what these words represent to you. Let's focus on the term "Depressive Disorder" and, for the purpose of understanding the term, we will assume you have been given that label. Because you have been told you have a depressive disorder, understanding the meaning of that label is important. As a wise bib-lical counselor, I would ask you questions like those that follow to determine what you know and understand about this diagnosis. You may want to answer them for yourself!

---

[9] *MacArthur Study Bible*, Thomas Nelson, Copyright 2013, Study Note on 2 Corinthians 10:7

Do you believe depression is a disease that causes you to feel sad, tired, disinterested in life, guilty, or suicidal?

Do you believe you have this disease because you inherited it from your father or mother?

Are you able to control your feelings?

Have you begun to neglect your responsibilities (e.g., staying home from work, not paying bills, not caring for children)? How often?

What do you do while avoiding responsibilities? (Do you stay in bed, cry, sleep, or drink alcohol?)

What are you thinking about when you feel sad, disinterested in life, or suicidal?

What problems result from avoiding responsibilities?

Would you like to understand what the Bible says about your thoughts and behavior, and what you can do about it?

Take some time and write down in your notebook all the feelings and behaviors you can think of that characterize you at this time. What words would you use to describe how you feel? Are you sad, grief stricken, despondent, mourning, hopeless, despairing, angry, lonely, or tired?

Read the following passages from the Bible and take notes about what you read.

- Deuteronomy 31:6
- Isaiah 26:3
- Isaiah 41:10
- Lamentations 3:21-24
- Psalm 43:4
- Psalm 46:1
- Psalm 69
- Psalm 51
- Psalm 32
- Psalm 38
- Psalm 45
- 2 Corinthians 4:16
- Hebrews 12:2

Did you find the phrase, "depressive disorder" in the Bible? No, but you did find adjectives like sorrow, grieved, and downcast that clearly describe the feelings, behavior, and mindset of a person who is suffering from what we would call depression.

When you define depression the way the Bible defines it, you are describing sinful thoughts, beliefs, desires, and behavior for which Christ died! There is a lot of hope there! When you begin to adopt biblical thinking and practice it in your behavior, you will see changes in your feelings. A behavior can be stopped and avoided because it is a choice. The choice begins with the desires of the heart.

On the other hand, when behavior is labeled as a disease, you are led to believe that you will have depressive disorder for the rest of your life, even if you never have another depressive episode. You are saddled with a medical diagnosis code, which in the medical realm may mean you have an illness from which you will never recover. You are now a victim of an illness. You have a problem that cannot be fixed, which takes away all hope. There is no victory there.

Christ died to give us victory over the flesh that drives us to be sinful in our thoughts and desires. I pray this brings you tremendous hope!

Understanding this is crucial because it means either a life of freedom in Christ or bondage to man-made terminology. Using worldly terminology traps people. In many cases, people who believe they are being kind are doing harm. Some might say it is cruel for you to be told that you are sinning. Truthfully, it is unkind when people do not tell you the truth; in fact, it is very unkind because you cannot deal with sinful behavior when it is labeled and excused as a disease.

It is helpful to define biblically the terms that psychology uses. Long before the psychological terms were invented, God knew the behaviors and had the remedy at hand. Consider these common words in the medical model and their biblical equivalents:

- Addiction—bondage to sin
- Attitude—spirit of one's heart or thoughts
- Alcoholic—drunkard
- Anger—selfish desires withheld
- Anxiety—fear; worry; lack of faith in God's love or care
- Can't forgive self—unbelief; insuffcient confidence in God's Word
- Co-dependent—idolatry; fear of man
- Complaining—murmuring; disputing; discontent
- Compulsive disorder—life-dominating sin; bondage to sin; guilt
- Depression—sorrow without hope
- Dysfunctional—sinning
- Ego—pride

- Emotional problem—thinking problem (the emotions are working fine)
- Frustrated—angry; interference blocks selfish goal; disappointed; cast down; discouraged
- Grief—sorrow, mourning
- Grudge—refusal to forgive
- In denial—self-deceived; deceitful heart
- Insane/unstable—double minded
- Insecure—fearful
- Mental health—spiritual health
- Mistake—sin
- Need—desire
- Overwhelmed—fainthearted
- Oppositional Defiant Disorder (ODD)—rebellion toward God's authority; anger
- Self-esteem—self-love, lover of self
- Self-image—self-judgment
- Self-pity—resentful; discontented; self-centered
- Suicide—self-murder

As long as you believe you bear no responsibility for your behavior or circumstances, you may not be able to receive help. How will you be able to clear your conscience and accept responsibility for your behavior if you think you are not responsible? If your thoughts are rooted in human reasoning or things that are in opposition to God's truth and wisdom, you will become confused in your heart and you will have diffculty embracing God's will or God's truth. When you define the terms biblically, it will help you begin to understand that such diagnoses are not life sentences, but only words that psychology has created to define behaviors. When you are willing to look at your ungodly actions, thoughts, and beliefs from a biblical perspective, you will begin to experience true freedom from enslavement to any sin. You must admit to God and to yourself that you have chosen to participate in sin.

Application of The Roots-and-Fruits Principle to Depression

Jesus said, "A tree is identified by its fruit. Make a tree good, and its fruit will be good. Make a tree bad, and its fruit will be bad."

Matthew 12:33 (NLT)

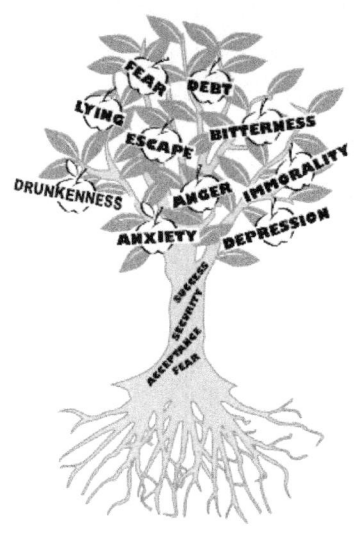

The quality of the fruit of any tree depends on the root system of that tree. The tree rooted in poor quality soil will have little nutrition to carry up through the trunk to the branches and leaves. The tree will be weak and susceptible to disease. The quality of its fruit will be poor. You could return year after year and pluck the poor fruit from the tree, but that would not change the health of the tree. The tree would remain sickly and vulnerable, bearing bad fruit. The only way to cause a tree to produce good fruit is to attend to the roots.

To make application to your life, if you address only your depressive feelings (fruit), you will be depressed again in a short time. There is a problem deeper down in your tree of life. Something has caused your fruit to be bad. You must address the root system. Deal with your depression by attacking the real causes (roots) in a biblical manner. You have to deal with the heart of your problem in order to overcome it. In the case of humanity, the root system on the tree is equal to the heart.

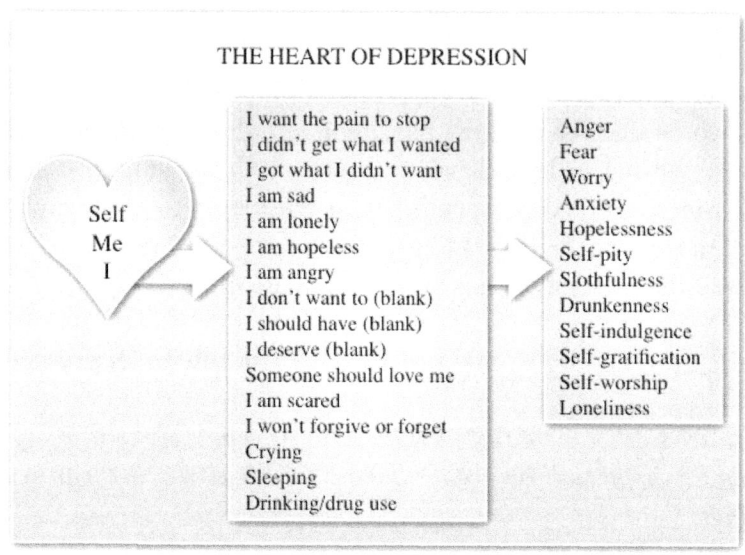

THE HEART OF DEPRESSION

Self
Me
I

I want the pain to stop
I didn't get what I wanted
I got what I didn't want
I am sad
I am lonely
I am hopeless
I am angry
I don't want to (blank)
I should have (blank)
I deserve (blank)
Someone should love me
I am scared
I won't forgive or forget
Crying
Sleeping
Drinking/drug use

Anger
Fear
Worry
Anxiety
Hopelessness
Self-pity
Slothfulness
Drunkenness
Self-indulgence
Self-gratification
Self-worship
Loneliness

If you have the fruit of depression, you need to ask yourself if you are focused on your wants, your perceived needs, your personal rights, your beliefs and desires. Thinking this way results in a self-centered, idolatrous heart, which is revealed by your thoughts, words, and actions.

Some of the actions of the depressed person:

If you are depressed, you may have come to believe you needed certain things or people to make you happy. Even though you may have gotten those things, you find you are still unhappy.

- Not going to work or doing nothing but work.
- Not communicating with friends and family.
- Not cooking or cleaning.
- Preferring to lie in bed all day and sleep or cry.
- Denying a problem.
- Overeating or starving.
- Getting drunk or high.

Self-focused motivations spurred on by the desires of the sinful heart will produce the kind of fruit you would expect—depression and discouragement.

Will biblical counseling cure your depression? It may surprise you that biblical counseling does not place a heavy focus on the fruit of depression. It is not profitable to simply pull the bad fruit off the tree, because new bad fruit will soon grow in its place. The depression you are experiencing is the result of the problem, not necessarily the problem itself. A biblical counselor will help you deal with your depression by examining the source of the feelings— your beliefs, desires, and thoughts; or, as the Bible says, your heart. Because the heart is set on pleasing self, your thoughts and actions are not naturally going to be like God's. This presents a dilemma because glorifying God is to be the goal of our lives. Depressed persons often struggle with the meaning of life, asking questions such as, "Why am I here?" The simple and straightforward answer to this question could change your life: You are here to glorify God (Isaiah 43:7).

God is glorified when the focus of your life changes from living for your own pleasure and glory, to living for His pleasure and glory.

As you address what is guiding and motivating your heart, you will learn to intentionally keep your mind focused on thoughts that are pleasing and edifying to God. This is the renewing of your mind.

Here are some ways you can begin to address your wrong thoughts and beliefs:

- Take every thought captive (2 Corinthians 10:5).
- Find hope in the Word (Proverbs 13:12; Colossians 1:27; Titus 2:11-13).
- Focus on praising and thanking God for His provisions and promises (Colossians 3:1-4; 2 Peter 1:4).
- Forgive those with whom you are angry (Mark 11:25-26; Ephesians 4:32; Colossians 3:13).
- Identify the idols in your life and turn away from them!
- Make it your desire to glorify God (Exodus 20:4; I John 5:21).
- Humble yourself (James 4:6-10).
- Identify your sinful responses to your circumstances and feelings and repent (Joel 2:12, 13; Romans 2:4; 2 Corinthians 7:10, 11).

If you are suffering with feelings of depression today, please understand that God is sovereign and is at work in your life. No matter how much you may not like what you are going through, your situation is not a mistake; it is a divine appointment. God is using this in the process of your progressive sanctification. He is in this trial with you and wants you to break free from your bondage. Do not fail to see yourself in the light of God's grace today.

Chapter 2
Mind Renewal Brings Heart Change

Do not be conformed any longer to the pattern of this world, but be transformed by the renewing of your mind.

Romans 12:2 (NKJ)

Mind renewal is especially important when dealing with depression. When your thoughts, beliefs, and desires are set on glorifying God, and you begin to do things, such as serving others, you may begin to experience relief from your depressive feelings. Even if you don't, you can still be confident God is being honored as you obey the commands to love and serve others.

♥*Heart Work*

Consider what God says about your reason for living. Take some time and do an internet search for Bible verses on "Why did He create me?"

Search the Scriptures and make a list of the reasons God says He made you. To get you started, look up 1 Corinthians 6:20.

Remind yourself daily of your spiritual identity. The book of Ephesians gives you some great clues about who you are in Christ. Examine the book in depth, especially the first three chapters. Take notes, use various translations, and look up words you don't know or understand online using the Blue Letter Bible, or in a concordance, such as Vine's or Strong's.

Do you know who you are in Christ? Check the Blue Letter Bible online or concordance for the following words and write out their definitions.

Justified
Sanctified
Called
Elect
Blameless
Holy

Memorize the Bible verses that reveal how these words apply to you.

Look for God at work in your circumstances. Examine the life of biblical characters such as David, Samuel, Ruth, Naomi, King Saul, Samson, Elijah, and Paul. These people were used by God and still testify to us today; how did they handle their crises and troubles?

Therefore, since we are surrounded by such a huge crowd of witnesses to the life of faith, let us strip off every weight that slows us down, especially the sin that so easily hinders our progress. And let us run with endurance the race that God has set before us. We do this by keeping our eyes on Jesus, on whom our faith depends from start to finish.
Hebrews 12:1-2a (NLT)

Do a study on what the Bible has to say about grumbling and complaining. Use both the Old and New Testaments.

Where is your focus today?

Instead of focusing on your feelings, focus on glorifying God. The goal of true change is to honor Jesus Christ in the midst of your circumstances. He is your answer. He is your comfort. He is your help in time of need. He is your light, your salvation, and your all in all. He is your hope.

Paul said in Philippians 3:7-8 (NLT):

> *I once thought all these things were so very important, but now I consider them worthless because of what Christ has done. Yes, everything else is worthless when compared with the priceless gain of knowing Christ Jesus my Lord. I have discarded everything else, counting it all as garbage, so that I may have Christ and become one with him.*

In Philippians 3:10, he said:

> *I want to know Christ and the power of his resurrection and the fellowship of sharing in his sufferings, becoming like him in his death.*

And in 1 Corinthians 2:2:

> *For I determined not to know anything among you except Jesus Christ and Him crucified.*

In Ephesians 1:16-19 (NIV), Paul prays for believers in this manner:

I have not stopped giving thanks for you, remembering you in my prayers. I keep asking that the God of our Lord Jesus Christ, the glorious Father, may give you the Spirit of wisdom and revelation, so that you may know him better. I pray also that the eyes of your heart may be enlightened in order that you may know the hope to which he has called you, the riches of his glorious inheritance in the saints, and his incomparably great power for us who believe.

Paul's single goal was Christ—to know Him, to glorify Him, and to teach others to do the same. John exhorted us to love God more than the world or its pleasures:

Stop loving this evil world and all that it offers you, for when you love the world, you show that you do not have the love of the Father in you. For the world offers only the lust for physical pleasure, the lust for everything we see, and pride in our possessions. These are not from the Father. They are from this evil world. And this world is fading away, along with everything it craves. But if you do the will of God, you will live forever.

1 John 2:15-17 (NLT)

Let us behave decently, as in the daytime, not in orgies and drunkenness, not in sexual immorality and debauchery, not in dissension and jealousy. Rather, clothe yourselves with the Lord Jesus Christ, and do not think about how to gratify the desires of the sinful nature.

Romans 13:13-14 (NIV)

Renewing your mind with Scripture will enable you to put off the sinful desires of the flesh. These not only include immoral desires but also selfish desires: the selfish desires that keep you focusing only on yourself and how you feel today.

Jesus replied: 'Love the Lord your God with all your heart and with all your soul and with all your mind.' This is the first and greatest commandment.

Matthew 22:37-38 (NIV)

Loving God with all your heart, soul, and mind is impossible apart from the working of the Holy Spirit. God, who is far above all rule and power, must always take first place. He reigns in glory, independent of you and me. To say you can "make" God number one, and "make" Jesus Christ "Lord," Indicates that you have a low view of God. God is already God and Jesus Christ is Lord (Phil. 2:10-11).

What must change is your understanding of who you are! As you understand your humble position before an Almighty God, your perspective changes on how you are to live life. As you begin to comprehend that you are here to serve Him (not the other way around), Matthew 22:39 becomes reality: "Love your neighbor as yourself."

The Problem of Self-Esteem

Many people who suffer with feelings of depression are told they have low self-esteem. They are often given worldly counsel that suggests they need to love themselves more, indulge themselves more.

I will address this more in the next chapter, but because we are defining things biblically, it is important to understand that what the world calls "low self-esteem," is considered to be pride. Jesus knew the propensity of the heart is to be self-focused and self-worshiping. This is why He told us to love others as much as we already love ourselves instead of telling us to love ourselves more.

It can be difficult for a depressed person to hear that they have no problem loving themselves. Many would say they even hate themselves! Depressed people justify irresponsibility, neglecting their personal hygiene, staying in bed, or doing harm to themselves (e.g., getting drunk, cutting), with their feelings of depression.

Putting Love your neighbor as yourself into action means serving others. God has graciously given us direction in His Word to know how to serve our fellow man. A short list follows:

Be kindly affectionate to one another with brotherly love, in honor giving preference to one another.
Romans 12:10 (NKJV)

Therefore let us not judge one another anymore, but rather resolve this, not to put a stumbling block or a cause to fall in our brother's way.
Romans 14:13 (NKJV)

Now may the God of patience and comfort grant you to be likeminded toward one another, according to Christ Jesus.
Romans 15:5 (NKJV)

I, therefore, the prisoner of the Lord, beseech you to walk worthy of the calling with which you were called, with all lowliness and gentleness, with longsuffering, bearing with one another in love, endeavoring to keep the unity of the Spirit in the bond of peace.
Ephesians 4:1-3 (NKJV)

Loving and serving others takes the focus off of you. There will be little opportunity for selfish desires when you are busy serving others. This activity is not to be used as a technique to avoid dealing biblically with your issues. It is an act of obedience to God done for the purpose of bringing Him glory.

Proverbs 4:23 (NLT) says, *Above all else, guard your heart, for it affects everything you do.* Notice that your heart affects everything you do. This verse makes it clear that what you think and believe controls what you do and how you act. I have found certain common heart attitudes that persist in people with depression. You have read about them briefly to this point. Look with me now in depth at how they are revealed in daily life.

Selfishness - looking within
+
glorifying God -

But do not avoid issues

Chapter 3
The Prideful Heart

Pride is a heart attitude that overflows into a person's motivation, decision-making, and actions. Pride is at the root of nearly every problem we struggle with in counseling!

The heart of pride is focused on self. Prideful people believe they deserve better than what life has brought them. They become sorrowful, resentful, and even jealous of other people and their successes. Pride breeds self-pity, which is a major component in depression that we will talk about in a later chapter. Typically, people who struggle with pride will live life based on how they feel and expect everyone else to accommodate them and adapt to their moods.

Two key characteristics of pride are independence and rebellion. It should not be too diffcult for you to understand why this is so. The truth is we all want our own way about things, and we usually will do almost anything to have it our way. The sinful nature leads us to desire independence, and we rebel at the thought of being under anyone's control or authority.

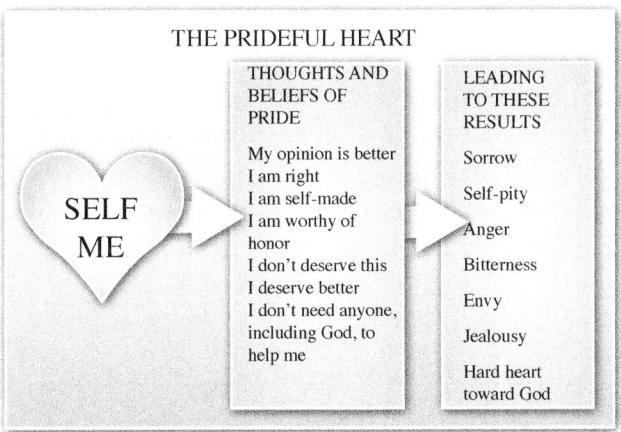

THE PRIDEFUL HEART

THOUGHTS AND BELIEFS OF PRIDE	LEADING TO THESE RESULTS
My opinion is better	Sorrow
I am right	
I am self-made	Self-pity
I am worthy of honor	Anger
I don't deserve this	Bitterness
I deserve better	
I don't need anyone, including God, to help me	Envy
	Jealousy
	Hard heart toward God

SELF ME

In his pride the wicked does not seek him; in all his thoughts there is no room for God. Psalm 10:4 (NIV)

In our hearts we say like Pharaoh did in Exodus 5:2, "Who is the Lord that I should obey Him?"

Looking at the Heart of Pride diagram, you can see that the thoughts, beliefs, and desires of a prideful person are focused on themselves. People infected by pride typically think so highly of themselves that they believe the world should revolve around them. The only thing important to prideful people is getting their needs met. It may be an emotional need, a desire for attention, or a resistance to conform to social norms in order to be seen as an individual.

The prideful person truly believes they deserve better than what God has given them; their thoughts are focused on what they feel they deserve or don't deserve. They think they are entitled to more than what they have simply because of who they are. They have a very high opinion of themselves, and think their conclusions and opinions are right or best. The world revolves around them, or, at least it should! There is little need for God on a practical level because the prideful person believes they have everything under control without God's help.

The results of these sinful heart attitudes are clear, and none of them are good. Prideful people struggle with bitterness, revenge, conceit, self-pity, a competitive nature, gossip, slander, and vanity. Those who have feelings of depression usually struggle with pride on a deeper level. They may not verbalize it, but underneath the depressive feelings are anger and self-pity because they do not believe they deserve the negative things that have befallen them and they think they deserve something better. It is as though they say, "God, this shouldn't be happening to me! Don't you know who I am?" They display a desire to be noticed, which is disguised as shyness. They typically have a lust for attention, approval, and praise. Those who attempt to build them up psychologically only assist them in further self-indulgence.

♥ Heart Work

People who are burdened with feelings of depression question God's authority in their lives. Would you say you have done so?

Have you challenged God's wisdom in the circumstances of your life?

Do you think/believe you deserve better/more because of who you are/what you do for God?

How many of the thoughts, beliefs, and desires in the Heart of Pride diagram do you relate to?

Do you understand God's thoughts on the sin of pride? The truth is you cannot remain full of pride because God hates it.

All who fear the LORD will hate evil. That is why I hate pride, arrogance, corruption, and perverted speech. Proverbs 8:13 (NLT)

The heart of pride brings devastating consequences that God ordains: a hardened heart and other consequences of this sin.

Scripture shows us the results of pride through the examples of two kings: King Nebuchadnezzar and King Herod. They both became prideful and consequently were humbled by God.

But when [Nebuchadnezzar's] heart became arrogant and hardened with pride, he was deposed from his royal throne and stripped of his glory. He was driven away from people and given the mind of an animal; he lived with the wild donkeys and ate grass like cattle; and his body was drenched with the dew of heaven, until he acknowledged that the Most High God is sovereign over the kingdoms of men and sets over them anyone he wishes.

Daniel 5:20-21 (NIV)

King Nebuchadnezzar lived like an animal until he came to his senses and repented of his sin. God then restored the kingdom to him.

On the appointed day Herod, wearing his royal robes, sat on his throne and delivered a public address to the people. They shouted, "This is the voice of a god, not of a man." Immediately, because Herod did not give praise to God, an angel of the Lord struck him down, and he was eaten by worms and died.

Acts 12:2-23 (NIV)

Pride will cause you to harden your heart toward God. Consequently, God will not allow you to prosper. He will bring you dishonor, which is the last thing a prideful person wants.

When pride comes, then comes disgrace, but with humility comes wisdom.

Proverbs 11:2 (NIV)

Pride brings opposition from God. He will not share His glory with anyone or anything.

All of you, clothe yourselves with humility toward one another, because, "God opposes the proud but gives grace to the humble."

1 Peter 5:5 (NIV)

The prideful person is self-deceived.

For if anyone thinks himself to be something, when he is nothing, he deceives himself.

Galatians 6:3 (NKJV)

As I said in a previous chapter, prideful people are often mistakenly diagnosed with low self-esteem because their actions and attitudes appear to be self-depreciating. Low self-esteem is defined as "a person's belief regarding the degree to which he is worthy of praise."

Curing the Prideful Heart

There is only one cure for the prideful heart, and that is to develop humility. You can begin this process by going through the

52

list of your prideful thoughts, beliefs, desires and actions. Then confess, or admit to God that you struggle with the sin of pride. Confession is agreeing with God that what you have done is wrong. You might pray a simple prayer similar to this one:

Dear Heavenly Father, I confess to you that I struggle with the sin of pride in my heart and my life. This pride leads me to act out selfish desires and is hurtful to other people. I ask for the help of the Holy Spirit to change my heart so that I become selfless and learn to serve others as I consider them before myself. Thank You for the forgiveness that is mine through the Lord Jesus Christ, and I pray these things for Your glory. In Jesus name, Amen.

THE HUMBLE HEART

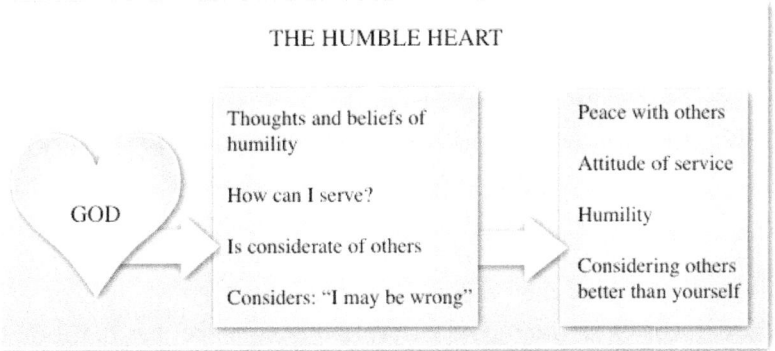

Confession and prayer are excellent first steps, but other action is necessary. You must take seriously the commands of Scripture regarding humility, a denial of self. Humility is lived out as you learn to consider others better than yourself.

For by the grace given me I say to every one of you: Do not think of yourself more highly than you ought, but rather think of yourself with sober judgment, in accordance with the measure of faith God has given you.

Romans 12:3 (NIV)

There is no better example of humility than the Lord Jesus Christ. Jesus was the ultimate example of humility. He was God, yet He condescended to come to earth as a human being. He denied

Himself and deprived Himself of heaven and all its glory for 33 years for you and me.

> *Have this attitude in yourselves which was also in Christ Jesus, who, although He existed in the form of God, did not regard equality with God a thing to be grasped, but emptied Himself, taking the form of a bond-servant, and being made in the likeness of men. Being found in appearance as a man, He humbled Himself by becoming obedient to the point of death, even death on a cross.*
>
> Philippians 2:5-8 (NASB)

Because our goal is to become like Jesus in character and attitude, we are to practice how Jesus lived His life. Jesus was described as "meek and lowly." Meekness is an internal quality that comes with humility. As a heart attitude, it is the opposite of pride. The one meek in heart is not concerned about self and readily puts the interest of others before his or her own interests.

Being meek does not mean weak; in fact, it means just the opposite. It takes great strength to be humble before God and others. This really goes against the grain of the sinful nature. It is possible, however, for even the most prideful person to become humble. Humility is a fruit of the Spirit, and God joyfully responds to those who desire it.

> *Then he (Jesus) said to the crowd, "If any of you wants to be my follower, you must put aside your selfish ambition, shoulder your cross daily, and follow me. If you try to keep your life for yourself, you will lose it. But if you give up your life for me, you will find true life. And how do you benefit if you gain the whole world but lose or forfeit your own soul in the process?"*
>
> Luke 9:23-25 (NLT)

> *Live in harmony with one another. Do not be proud, but be willing to associate with people of low position. Do not be conceited.*
>
> Romans 12:16 (NIV)

My favorite passage of Scripture regarding humility is found in Philippians, Chapter 2.

Do nothing out of selfish ambition or vain conceit, but in humility consider others better than yourselves. Each of you should look not only to your own interests, but also to the interests of others. Philippians 2:3-4 (NIV)

The prideful person must begin to look at others as better, and more important than themselves. Other's thoughts, desires, needs, wants, opinions, all become more important to you than your own. You begin to have a real view of yourself that is based on the Scriptures. Rather than elevating yourself and having a high opinion of yourself, you will quickly understand how despicable you actually are apart from the grace and mercy of Christ.

Humility will develop as you internalize the truth that nothing in the life of a Christian is to be about "me." It is all about Jesus Christ and Him only. You cannot possibly dwell on "what I want" or "what I think is better or right," with a biblical view of yourself.

♥*Heart Work*

Select several Scriptures on pride and humility found in this chapter, write them in your notebook, and begin to memorize them.

Ask the Lord to help you become more aware of your prideful thoughts throughout the day. When you have prideful thoughts, immediately confess them and ask the Lord to help you to respond humbly instead.

Be vigilant in submitting your thoughts, beliefs, and desires to the Holy Spirit in prayer and ask His help in recognizing pride.

On a practical level, do one thing a day for someone you ordinarily would avoid, someone you think you are better than.

Go out of your way to help another person.

Give up something you want to do for the sake of another's pleasure.

Consider the opinion of a person you think is "beneath you" and follow his or her suggestion.

When you begin to practice these suggestions, you will find joy returning to your life. Your world will open up to others as your heart opens up. As you continue to place others above yourself, your desire to serve them will grow, and life will become fulfilling again.

This will help you in overcoming your feelings of depression on several levels! God is pleased when a sinner repents of sin and changes the attitudes of the heart. The knowledge that you are glorifying God will bring joy into your life. You will be thinking of other people and spending less time dwelling on you.

Chapter 4
The Angry Heart

A wise man fears the LORD and shuns evil, but a fool is hot-headed and reckless. A quick-tempered man does foolish things, and a crafty man is hated.

Proverbs 14:16-17 (NIV)

An angry man stirs up dissension, and a hot-tempered one commits many sins.

Proverbs 29:22 (NIV)

In my years of counseling the one thing that has been consistent is that depressed people are angry people. My husband Larry, also a counselor, describes the reasons people typically become sinfully angry: You are either angry about something you got and didn't want, or you are angry about something you wanted and didn't get.

What did you get that you did not want?

What did you want that did you did not get?

We live in a society that screams constantly about "rights". Women champion their "right to choose"; homosexuals fight for the rights of marriage; children claim a right to privacy, and husbands claim a right to sexual relations. When our perceived rights are vio-lated we become angry, but how many of these rights are biblical?

♥ *Heart Work*
Compare some of the common perceived rights listed below against your own belief system.
Make a mark next to those you believe are your rights.

- •Right to have and express personal opinions
- •Right to be respected
- •Right to be understood
- •Right to have good health
- •Right to be appreciated
- •Right to be treated fairly

- •Right to earn and use money
- •Right to belong, to be loved, to be accepted
- •Right to be supported
- •Right to make your own decisions
- •Right to determine your own future
- •Right to be considered worthwhile and important
- •Right to be protected and cared for
- •Right to have the job you want
- •Right to have fun
- •Right to raise your children your way
- •Right to security and safety
- •Right to have others obey you
- •Right to have your own way
- •Right to be free from diffculties and problems

This list is adapted from Wayne Mack's Homework Manual for Biblical Counselors, Volume 1

How many of these have you claimed as your "right"?

How many have you been denied?

Do you think being denied what you think and believe are your rights might be a partial cause for anger and depression?

Find Scripture that will support your beliefs that you are entitled to the "rights" you have claimed. Write the chapter and verse reference next to each "right" you have claimed.

Yes, many of the things in the list are promoted in our culture as your rights; however, very few of the things you claimed as your rights are found in Scripture. Most of them are attitudes of entitlement you have adopted as a result of your prideful heart attitudes. Denial of what you have claimed as your rights leads you to respond in anger.

Look at the diagram below. It shows that feelings of anger are generally (wrongly) handled in one of two ways: Blowing up (screaming, ranting raving, hollering, hitting, breaking things, driving too fast or recklessly); or clamming up (quietly internalizing the emotions, seething). One of these has become your default or habitual response when angry.

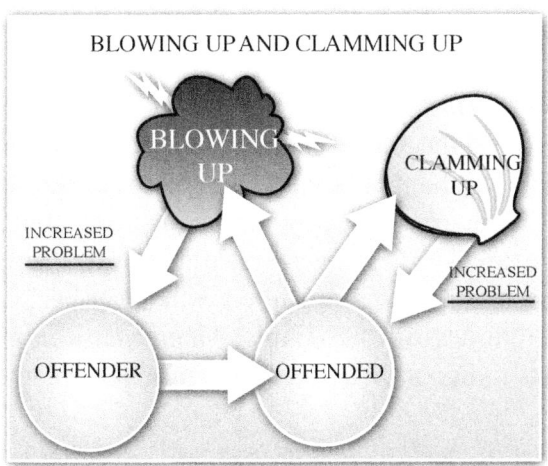

BLOWING UP AND CLAMMING UP

The one who blows up aims the energy of anger at someone or something that may or may not have anything to do with the problem at hand. Blowing up is costly in many ways. The display of sinful anger fractures relationships, frightens people, can lead to physical harm, can be costly due to property damage, and may even lead to the loss of employment. These consequences cause more problems for the angry person.

Those who clam up usually clamp down on the emotion and stuff the anger inside. Sometimes the anger festers inside for weeks and even years. I have had counselees who still carry anger for events that occurred decades ago. (Christian women are often taught that it is not acceptable to display anger and that it is more spiritual to hold it inside. Somehow, it's not considered to be sinful anger if it's not explosive anger, but that is just not true. All anger has to be dealt with!) Over time, stuffing all that anger inside can lead to digestive, muscular, and other physical problems such as migraines. Your body is not intended to carry the stress of unresolved anger.

♥ *Heart Work*
Which is your default response—Are you one who blows up or one who clams up?

What consequences of blowing up or clamming up have you experienced...

Physically?	Spiritually?
Emotionally?	Relationally?

Righteous and Unrighteous Anger

Understand, the Bible does not prohibit becoming angry. God has given you the emotion of anger and its energy is intended to be used in solving the problem at hand. Not all anger is sinful. The Lord Jesus Christ experienced and demonstrated anger, but in no way did He ever sin in His anger. When Jesus saw the moneychangers in the temple of God, he was filled with anger because they were violating the holiness of the temple. Their wickedness filled Jesus with righteous indignation and drove Him to action.

Jesus entered the Temple and began to drive out the merchants and their customers. He knocked over the tables of the money changers and the stalls of those selling doves. "It is written," he said to them, "My house will be called a house of prayer, but you are making it a den of robbers."

Matthew 21:12-13 (NIV)

He looked around at them angrily, because he was deeply disturbed by their hard hearts.

Mark 3:5 (NLT)

Like Jesus, you are able to express righteous anger. Anger is righteous and justified when you see social or personal evils such as injustice prevail, or when you see God's holy standards being violated in abortion or another kind of homicide, sexual trafficking, or exploitation of children. This kind of anger does not have its root in "self" because the one being sinned against is God and His standards and principles, not you. It is anger on behalf of another who has been wronged.

That, however, is rarely the kind of anger we demonstrate. Most anger is generated in a heart that has self-centered thoughts, beliefs, and desires. These sinful heart attitudes are rooted in a prideful desire for control.

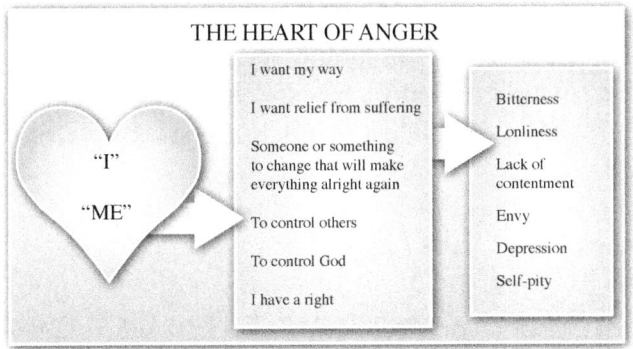

THE HEART OF ANGER

"I"

"ME"

I want my way

I want relief from suffering

Someone or something to change that will make everything alright again

To control others

To control God

I have a right

Bitterness

Lonliness

Lack of contentment

Envy

Depression

Self-pity

♥ Heart Work

Examine the above diagram. How many of the thoughts, beliefs, and desires are familiar to you?

One of my counseling goals is to help my angry counselees understand that much of the problem of depression is wrapped up in their desire to control other people and ultimately, to control God.

Think about how often you become angry when God makes decisions you don't like. Do you attempt to manipulate or bargain with God to get your own way?

Do you internalize your anger, resigning yourself to being under the thumb of one who is more powerful than you are? Write your usual response and your thoughts in your notebook.

Because angry people cannot make God do things their way, they often become full of self-pity. God's sovereign will violates their perceived rights.

Such thoughts reveal a prideful, idolatrous heart and lead to anger, bitterness, and eventually feelings of depression. In fact, depression is anger turned inward. When a person becomes angry and does not repent of it or address it biblically, depression can be a result.

One common denominator in angry people is that they do not understand the sovereignty of God; or they do understand it but they refuse to humbly accept it. God is in absolute control of all the circumstances of your life. Though you may be angered by these circumstances, because they most likely rearrange your plans, you ought to welcome them as friends.

God intends to use the things in your life to help you to become more like Christ. This should be an immense comfort to you. God is the sovereign God of the universe, and He does what He wants with what is His, and it is always good. In fact, it is always very good!

The Bible has this to say to those who become angry at the will of a sovereign God:

But who are you, O man, to talk back to God? "Shall what is formed say to him who formed it, 'Why did you make me like this?"

Romans 9:20 (NIV)

Who is this that questions my wisdom with such ignorant words?

Job 38:2 (NLT)

Then the LORD said to Job, "Do you still want to argue with the Almighty? You are God's critic, but do you have the answers?"

Job 40:1-2 (NLT)

The earth is the LORD'S, and everything in it. The world and all its people belong to him.

Psalm 24:1 (NLT)

I, the LORD, search all hearts and examine secret motives. I give all people their due rewards, according to what their actions deserve.

Jeremiah 17:10 (NLT)

Curing the Angry Heart

There can be only one godly response to sinful anger: Repentance that leads to change. You must begin to renew your mind by studying what Scripture says regarding anger. Consider the biblical commands we are given regarding what we are to do with this God-given emotion:

But now you must rid yourselves of all such things as these: anger, rage, malice, slander, and filthy language from your lips.

Colossians 3:8 (NIV)

♥ *Heart Work*

Look up the following verses in the Blue Letter Bible and click on the interlinear tab. Look at the meanings for all of the words related to anger in each verse. Write out the aspects of sinful anger that you know you struggle with.

Colossians 3:8
Ephesians 4:31
Galatians 5:20

Get rid of all bitterness, rage and anger, brawling and slander, along with every form of malice.

Ephesians 4:31 (NIV)

My dear brothers, take note of this: Everyone should be quick to listen, slow to speak and slow to become angry, for man's anger does not bring about the righteous life that God desires.

James 1:19-20 (NIV)

Don't say, "I will get even for this wrong." Wait for the LORD to handle the matter.

Proverbs 20:22 (NLT)

Anger is a sin that leads to other sins, including wrath, envy, jealousy, and murder. Put these things away from you!

When striving to overcome old responses, you may wrestle with your thoughts and emotions, because you have learned a habit. It will take some time for you to master new responses, but be encouraged. You can see change beginning today!

Don't sin by letting anger gain control over you. Don't let the sun go down while you are still angry.

Ephesians 4:26 (NLT)

God has not asked us to do something He has not equipped us to do. Since God's Word says "Be angry but don't sin", it must be possible to do just that. The encouraging truth is that you do not have to sin when you are angry.

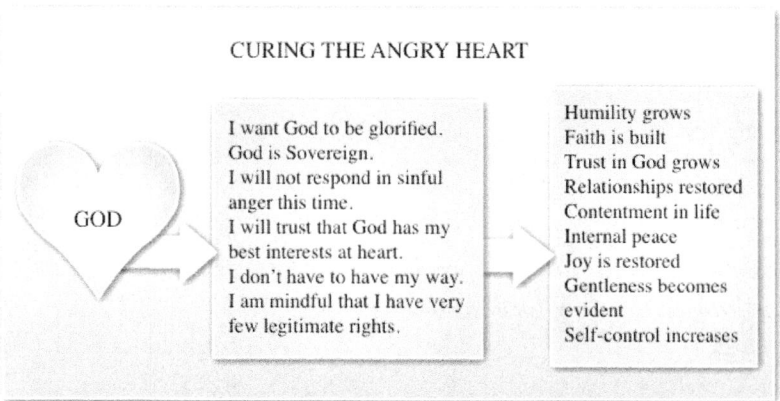

CURING THE ANGRY HEART

GOD

I want God to be glorified.
God is Sovereign.
I will not respond in sinful anger this time.
I will trust that God has my best interests at heart.
I don't have to have my way.
I am mindful that I have very few legitimate rights.

Humility grows
Faith is built
Trust in God grows
Relationships restored
Contentment in life
Internal peace
Joy is restored
Gentleness becomes evident
Self-control increases

Heart change begins when you acknowledge before God all the ways that you struggle with sinful anger by confessing it to Him. You might pray a prayer similar to this:

Dear gracious Father, I confess to You that I struggle with sinful anger, and Lord, that I sin deeply in my anger. Help me to see this sin the way You see it. I confess to you that I have hurt others by my angry words and actions. I ask You to give me the courage to confess my sin to those I have hurt and to seek their forgiveness. By Your grace, dear Lord, I commit to changing my ways. Help me to overcome this sinful pattern in my life. I choose to put off my sinful anger and to learn and practice new behaviors by the power of the Holy Spirit. Thank You for the forgiveness that is mine through the Lord Jesus Christ. I pray these things in Jesus' name, Amen.

Think of how your life would change if you changed your thoughts, beliefs and desires to those like the ones in the diagram above. Desiring to glorify God above all will help you make the greatest changes in your life. You will begin to "check" your thoughts and your words before you sin. You will begin to be more aware of the thoughts that feed your anger, and the selfish and sinful desires you harbor in your heart.

As in the diagram below, if you are accustomed to blowing up when you're angry, you must learn to enact new responses that will direct the energy of anger toward fixing the problem instead of using your anger to hurt people and damage or destroy property.

If you typically clam up or bury your anger, you must begin to appropriately verbalize what has caused you to become angry and then take steps to correct the problem.

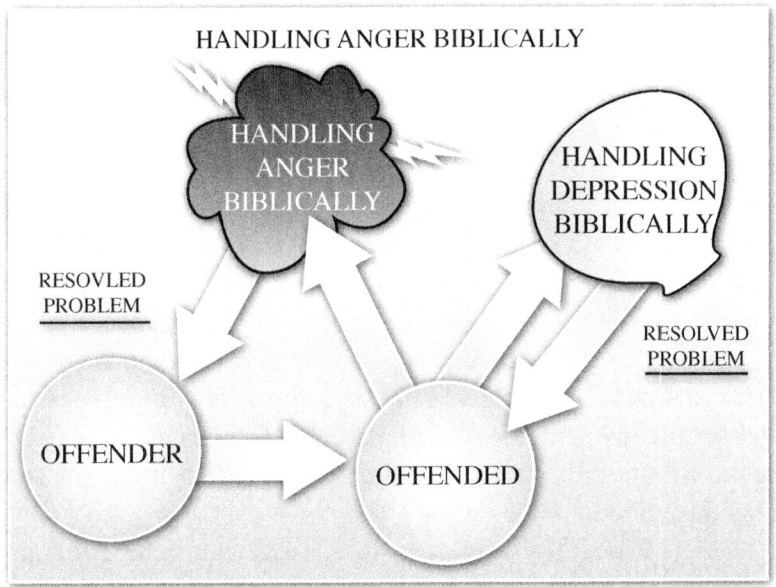

Make a plan to respond differently. The things that anger you are likely repetitive. Perhaps it is that person who speaks to you disrespectfully. Maybe it is being stuck in traffic while you are late to work or school. It is very important, while you are new at working to overcome sinful anger, that you write out a literal plan for change in detail. I encourage you to write out a script with your new responses and when the situation arises, bring it out and work the plan.

I have given this counsel numerous times and sadly, most people choose to make the plan only in their mind. I promise you that is a plan that will fail. In the moment when sinful anger wants to rear its ugly head, it is far too difficult to enact a plan you only have in your mind. Take the time and write it out in detail.

At first you may find it diffcult to respond appropriately to anger, but it will become easier as you grow in your understanding of the righteous responses to anger and as you continue to practice the right responses. There may be many failures at first, but don't be discouraged, my friend! God is a patient and loving Father, and He will bring you many opportunities to succeed.

I would also encourage you to grow in your understanding of the sovereignty of God. God is completely trustworthy and is completely aware of the circumstances that caused you to become angry. As you gain even a rudimentary understanding of the sovereignty of God, it will totally revolutionize your thinking. You will begin to understand that true wisdom comes from looking at life from God's perspective. When we can see problems and frustrations of life from God's perspective, they take on an entirely different hue. You will begin to see God's hand working and moving in your situations. Having your own way will no longer seem as important to you because you will be seeing things out of an entirely different set of lenses. When you look at life from God's perspective, you have taken yourself out of the center of your universe.

You **can** experience heart change in your response to anger. I know it is possible because I put these principles into place in my own life and have experienced change that brings God glory. It took time, and I am still a work in progress, however I have grown and changed tremendously over the years.

Be warned, if you choose not to deal with your sinful anger, it will not just go away. Anger becomes more deeply entrenched and leads us to the next sinful heart attitude that many depressed people must address: Bitterness.

The Bitter Heart

When anger is not addressed biblically, it is allowed to fester. Over time it becomes bitterness. Bitterness is unresolved, unforgiven anger and resentment. It is the result of anger changing from an experience to a belief. The emotion of bitterness is seething and constant. Bitterness is sin. Bitter people carry the same physical and emotional burdens as angry people, but to a greater extent.

Bitterness is a deep cesspool of rotten emotion that burrows deep into the soul. Don't be deceived, you cannot fool around with bitterness and expect it not to own you. Many people do not see bitterness as sin, but as the justifiable result of something that has happened to them. Someone has hurt them, abused them, or disrespected them. Most people who are bitter will argue that they have the right to be so. Bitterness is justified by claiming that others are responsible for it: "Under my circumstances, can you blame me?"

The sinful actions and attitudes of bitterness are masked by righteous indignation and therefore seem justifiable. The person feels so justified in their bitterness they do not want to see the effect on their relationships.

♥ *Heart Work*
Is there someone in your life with whom you have unresolved anger?

Do you think about how justified you are for feeling about them the way you do? Explain your answer.

How much time do you spend thinking about how others have hurt you?

Are you able to quickly call to mind how you have been hurt?

Have you talked to others about what this person has done to you? Others who are not a part of the problem or a part of the solution?

Do you find yourself mulling over ways you would like to get even with the person who hurt you?

Watch out that no bitter root of unbelief rises up among you, for whenever it springs up, many are corrupted by its poison. Hebrews 12:15 (NLT)

Hebrews 12:15 is one of the most common passages in Scripture used to warn against the emotional state of bitterness. It reflects the idea of a rotten taste, like sucking on a lemon or an unsweetened grapefruit. Roots were used in Bible times (and derivatives are today) as medicine or food. However, sometimes roots were poisonous and when consumed the result would be sickness and or even death. That's the picture Scripture gives of a bitter root.

Bitterness hardens your heart on the inside and your features on the outside.

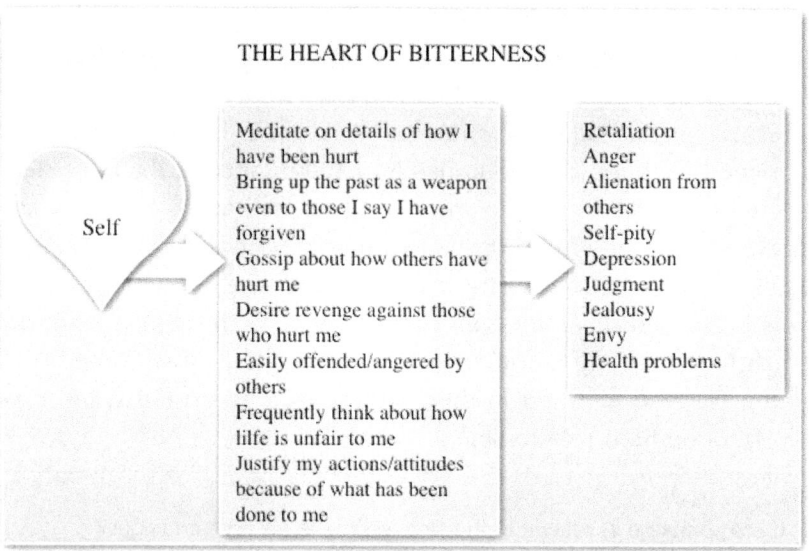

THE HEART OF BITTERNESS

| Self | Meditate on details of how I have been hurt
Bring up the past as a weapon even to those I say I have forgiven
Gossip about how others have hurt me
Desire revenge against those who hurt me
Easily offended/angered by others
Frequently think about how lilfe is unfair to me
Justify my actions/attitudes because of what has been done to me | Retaliation
Anger
Alienation from others
Self-pity
Depression
Judgment
Jealousy
Envy
Health problems |

As you reflect on the bitterness of your own heart, you may see your own thoughts, beliefs, and desires reflected in the diagram above.

How many of the consequences of bitterness are you experiencing in your own life?

Please understand, bitterness does not affect only you. It affects everyone with whom you come into contact. That is the defiling nature of bitterness.

In the book of Ruth, we read about Naomi (which means pleasant), the wife of Elimelech. Elimelech took his wife and two sons down from Bethlehem to the country of Moab because there was a famine in the land. While living in Moab, the sons took wives named Ruth and Orpah from among the native people. Elimelech and his two sons died in Moab and left Naomi, Ruth, and Orpah to fend for themselves.

When news came that the famine in the land of Judah had lifted, Naomi decided to return home to her own people. The three women set out together, but on the way, Naomi gave the young women the freedom to return home to their own people.

"No," they said. "We want to go with you to your people."
But Naomi replied, "Why should you go on with me? Can I still

68

*give birth to other sons who could grow up to be your husbands?
No, my daughters, return to your parents' homes, for I am too
old to marry again. And even if it were possible, and I were to
get married tonight and bear sons, then what? Would you wait
for them to grow up and refuse to marry someone else? No, of
course not, my daughters! Things are far more bitter for me than
for you, because the LORD himself has caused me to suffer."*

Ruth 1:10-14 (NLT)

Orpah did turn back, but Ruth was committed to Naomi and
to her God.

*So the two of them continued on their journey. When they came
to Bethlehem, the entire town was stirred by their arrival. "Is
it really Naomi?" the women asked. "Don't call me Naomi,"
she told them. "Instead, call me Mara, [meaning bitter] for the
Almighty has made life very bitter for me. I went away full, but
the LORD has brought me home empty. Why should you call
me Naomi when the LORD has caused me to suffer and the Almighty has sent such tragedy?"*

Ruth 1:19-21 (NLT)

What do you suppose it was that caused the whole town to
stir? Could it have been Naomi's appearance? Do you wonder if
they could see the changes that had taken place inside her heart, on
her face? Note the things Naomi says in verses 19-21:

*"Things are far more bitter for me than for you, because the
LORD himself has caused me to suffer." And ". . . call me Mara,
for the Almighty has made life very bitter for me. I went away
full, but the LORD has brought me home empty. Why should you
call me Naomi when the LORD has caused me to suffer and the
Almighty has sent such tragedy?"*

Naomi blames God for making her life bitter and empty. All
she can see is that she no longer has what she loved. Her bitterness
reflects a heart of unbelief in the justice and sovereignty of God.

She is holding on to the anger for what has been done to her and is standing in judgment over God. In the entire text, we see nothing of Naomi's quest to understand the purposes of God in her suffering. We only read that she is angry and bitter for what she has lost.

♥ *Heart Work*

Do you see yourself in Naomi? Do you think you are now "empty" when you once were "full"?

Who do you blame for your emptiness and loss?

How have you suffered as a result of your bitterness?

Have you benefitted in any way (physically, emotionally, spiritually) from being bitter?

Perhaps you struggle with the same type of bitterness as Naomi did. Sometimes women and men who have lost children to illness or accident blame God for their loss. "God, how could you take my beloved child from me? Don't You know how much I loved him? How could You do this to me?"

Left-behind spouses become bitter against their former husband or wife who is experiencing happiness in a new relationship while they sit at home raising the children from their former marriage. "God, don't You see how much I am struggling to raise these kids while he is out living the highlife? How can you let him get away with this? I am the one who was faithful, and now I am the one who is miserable while he has it made! Don't you care about me? Why aren't you punishing him?"

The honest businessman sees a crooked businessman prospering, while he flounders. "God, how can You stand by and let this happen? I am an honest businessman, and my business is failing! How can You let him get away with such thievery? I have a wife and kids to feed, God, why are you doing this to me?"

The childless couple is bitter when they see families with several children and they cannot seem to have even one. "God, why don't You let us have even one child when these other people have so many! It isn't fair that we can't have even one child to love while so many are being aborted and abandoned! God, why are You doing this to us?"

♥ Heart Work
What has happened in your life that has caused you to become bitter? Write it out in your journal.

You become bitter out of a belief that God will not punish the people who hurt you, that God does not hear your plea, or that He does not care about your plight. Since God is apparently not going to intervene in your circumstances, you stand in as judge, jury, and executioner in the lives of other people.

What has led you to become bitter? Do you see that it has become a circular pattern? The more you dwell on what has been done to you, the injustice you have suffered, or the loss you have incurred, the deeper the root of bitterness goes. You already know that carrying around a load of bitterness is exhausting. Bitterness hardens your heart on the inside and your features on the outside. It also defiles those around you because it is contagious.

♥ Heart Work
Looking back, can you see the circular pattern of bitterness in your life? Write it out in detail in your journal.

How has your bitterness affected those around you? If you are unsure, ask those closest to you for their input. When you do, be prepared to hear some difficult things!

Curing the Bitter Heart

Do you want the cure for bitterness? You must understand that the only cure for bitterness and anger is forgiveness.

Bitterness is focused on what has been done to you. To break up bitterness, you must also be willing to look at what you have done to others. Your task is to admit what your responsibility is in the matter, to get the log out of your own eye prior to examining your neighbor's eye.

And why worry about a speck in your friend's eye when you have a log in your own? How can you think of saying, 'Let me help you get rid of that speck in your eye,' when you can't see past the log in your own eye? Hypocrite! First get rid of the log from your own eye; then perhaps you will see well enough to deal with the speck in your friend's eye."

Matthew 7:3-5 (NLT)

The examination process begins right here at home. Start with yourself and seek God's help in revealing the contents of your heart in relation to how you have sinned against others. Pray as David did before you begin:

Search me, O God, and know my heart; test me and know my thoughts. Point out anything in me that offends you, and lead me along the path of everlasting life.

Psalm 139:23-24 (NLT)

♥ *Heart Work*
Take this time to "go logging" in your own eye. Prayerfully begin to search your own heart with respect to the bitterness you are harboring. BE SPECIFIC and DETAILED and list your personal sin. This is a time of self-examination before the Lord. You may be tempted to be very general, but I am encouraging you to dig deep and allow the Lord to begin to whack away at the root of bitterness you have grown.

There needs to be a willingness on your part to forsake your sin of bitterness.

Get rid of all bitterness, rage, anger, harsh words, and slander, as well as all types of malicious behavior. And be kind to one another, tenderhearted, forgiving one another, even as God in Christ forgave you.

Ephesians 4:31-32 (NLT)

Confession of your own sin and repentance for that sin must first take place in your heart. Then you must seek for other relationships to be healed and restored.

Forgiveness

Forgiving others is not an option for the Christian; it's required, and it is step number one in removing bitterness. We are commanded to forgive on the basis of the forgiveness we've received.

> *Since God chose you to be the holy people whom he loves, you must clothe yourselves with tenderhearted mercy, kindness, humility, gentleness, and patience. You must make allowance for each other's faults and forgive the person who offends you. Remember, the Lord forgave you, so you must forgive others.*
> Colossians 3:12-13 (NLT)

Some of Jesus's last words were words of forgiveness. Perhaps no incident in the Bible illustrates forgiveness from the heart better than Luke 23:34. As the Son of God was being cruelly and unjustly crucified, the Romans who were performing the deed were casting lots for his garments, and He said, "Father, forgive them for they know not what they do." In other words, Father, don't hold this against them. Jesus, it would seem, was practicing the very teaching on forgiveness he'd shared with his disciples in Matt. 18:21-35:

73

Then Peter came and said to Him, "Lord, how often shall my brother sin against me and I forgive him? Up to seven times?" Jesus said to him, "I do not say to you, up to seven times, but up to seventy times seven."

Matthew 18:21-22 (NASB)

"Forgiveness is a lifting of the charge of guilt from another, a formal declaration of that fact and a promise (made and kept) never to remember the wrong against the person in the future."
—Jay Adams, Theology of Christian Counseling

Forgiveness is not a feeling. It is an act of faith. It's an act of the will that triumphs over the feeling to not be forgiving, and the desire to seek revenge or remain bitter. It's remembering that we ourselves are sinners who get into the kingdom because we have been forgiven on the basis of the abundance of grace we ourselves received.

We choose, like Joseph, like Esau, like Paul, like Stephen, and like Jesus to release the person who has hurt us from the sense of debt we are owed. It's like saying, "Offender, you do not owe me anything, nor will I personally punish you for what you did to me. I choose to forgive this debt just as I have been forgiven my enormous debts."

Finally, it is important to understand that forgiveness is a promise to not dwell on the incident mentally. Stop dwelling on it. Forgiveness is also a promise to not bring the offense up to the person as a weapon. It is also a promise not to bring it up to others. If you are still talking to others about it, you haven't forgiven. If you've forgiven, then drop it.

Forgiveness from the heart is nothing more, nothing less than living out the Gospel of Grace. If you are going to pattern your forgiveness after that of the Lord, then you will choose to remember no more the sin committed against you.

Let me assure you that withholding forgiveness does nothing to address or cure any of the wounds you carry. It does nothing to change the past, but it will affect your future.

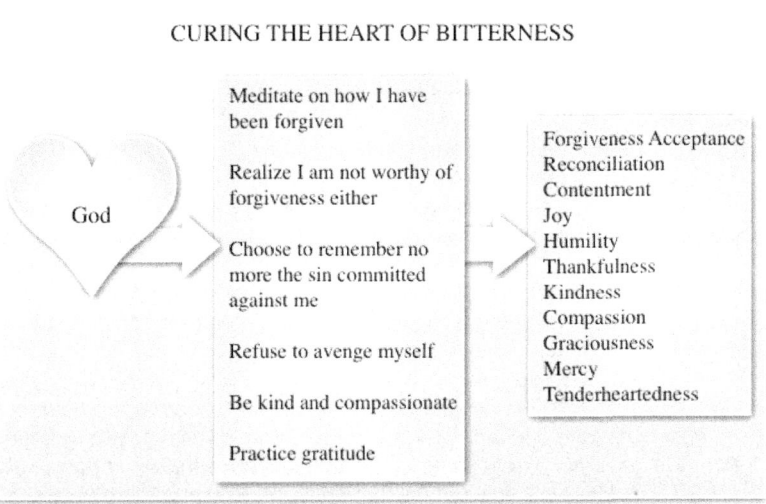

CURING THE HEART OF BITTERNESS

God

Meditate on how I have been forgiven

Realize I am not worthy of forgiveness either

Choose to remember no more the sin committed against me

Refuse to avenge myself

Be kind and compassionate

Practice gratitude

Forgiveness Acceptance
Reconciliation
Contentment
Joy
Humility
Thankfulness
Kindness
Compassion
Graciousness
Mercy
Tenderheartedness

But what if you are bitter toward God? What if you believe it is God who has hurt you and caused you pain? My dear friend, please take hold of this truth: God is the sovereign God of the entire universe. It is His, and He does with it what He wishes, and it is always good. In fact, it is always very good!

To believe you must forgive God for what you perceive He has done against you insinuates that God has sinned, and this cannot be. God is a loving, holy, and perfect, sinless God who does not make mistakes.

75

Naomi, as recorded in the book of Ruth, may have believed for a time that God somehow made a mistake in taking her husband and sons from her, for she said He "brought me back empty". It was no mistake, however. God was purposely unfolding His divine plan for humanity in Naomi's life and in the death of her loved ones. Take note, dear one, that if Naomi's son would have lived, Ruth would have remained his wife. Without the death of her husband, Ruth would not have been free to meet and marry Boaz, who became her kinsman redeemer. Ruth would not have given birth to their son, Obed, who became the father of Jesse, who is the father of David, from whose lineage comes the Christ.

Acceptance of hard things at the hand of a loving God is not easy. I encourage you to seek God in your circumstances and to trust that He is unfolding a divine plan that you cannot see right now, just as He did in the case of Naomi and Ruth. God's sovereignty is always balanced by His love, and He promises to bring good out of every tragedy and heartache.

♥ Heart Work
Have you blamed God for "bringing you back empty"?

Can you now see how what has happened to you can and will be used by God to bring about good things?

Can you understand and accept that while you may never see the end of the story, God has been unfolding a divine plan for you, and perhaps even those in your lineage?

> And we know that God causes everything to work together for the good of those who love God and are called according to his purpose for them. For God knew his people in advance, and he chose them to become like his Son, so that his Son would be the firstborn, with many brothers and sisters. Romans 8:28-29 (NLT)

Take some time and write out some possible good things (emotional, physical, spiritual) that can come from what you have experienced and are working through.

Chapter 5
The Self-Pitying Heart

Self-pity is a component of depression and another facet of anger. The heart of self-pity believes "I am entitled," "I deserve," and "God is so unfair." When the desires of your heart are not met, you tend to become angry with God and others for not meeting your perceived needs. You may think that troubles, hardships, and disappointments should not happen to you, that you are somehow above the normal issues of life.

The Self-Pitying Heart

♥ *Heart Work*
Have you been thinking thoughts like these?

Take a moment and write out additional thoughts like these that you have been having.

When things go wrong and times get hard, your thinking becomes focused on the problems you are facing. This feeds your sadness, perhaps to the point where you may become incapable of action and sometimes feel like you want to die.

A person who is feeling depressed will consistently speak of all that is wrong in their life, and how it affects them, with little or no hope of resolution. Their problem is amplified and appears bigger than life.

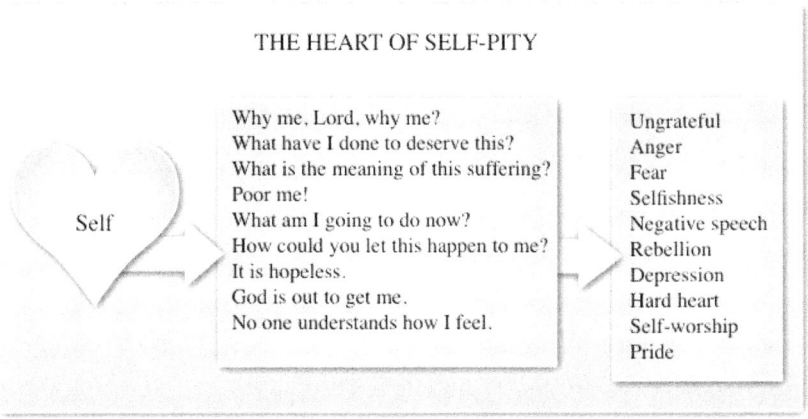

THE HEART OF SELF-PITY

| Self | Why me, Lord, why me?
What have I done to deserve this?
What is the meaning of this suffering?
Poor me!
What am I going to do now?
How could you let this happen to me?
It is hopeless.
God is out to get me.
No one understands how I feel. | Ungrateful
Anger
Fear
Selfishness
Negative speech
Rebellion
Depression
Hard heart
Self-worship
Pride |

The Bible teaches us that what comes out of the mouth reveals the condition of the heart; therefore, we can conclude that speech is the easiest method of determining self-pity. As you look at the diagram on the previous page, do you recall asking questions or making statements like these?

This kind of thinking becomes a miserable mindset, a completely distorted pattern of thinking, seeing, and feeling. After a time, the pattern becomes a sick way of life that you may recognize is not helpful, but is in fact harmful, yet now you just can't seem to stop it.

What you must realize is that if your speech is consistently negative and focused on all that is wrong in your life, you have created a heart of ingratitude and self-pity. You may want to believe that you can think ungrateful thoughts and speak of everything you lack without suffering discouragement and depression, but you have become self-deceived.

♥ *Heart Work*
What negative statements do you find you have stuck on "repeat"? Write them in your notebook.

God has kindly given us some biblical examples that we can turn to as we struggle to understand this intense feeling and state of mind that we call self-pity. The Old Testament prophet Jonah struggled with self-pity when he realized that God was not going to destroy the city of Ninevah. Some commentaries suggest Jonah was very concerned about how he would appear to the Ninevites because everything he predicted regarding their destruction was not going to happen.

This change of plans upset Jonah, and he became very angry. So he complained to the LORD about it:

"Didn't I say before I left home that you would do this, LORD? That is why I ran away to Tarshish! I knew that you were a gracious and compassionate God, slow to get angry and filled with unfailing love. I knew how easily you could cancel your plans for destroying these people. Just kill me now, LORD! I'd rather

*be dead than alive" . . . The LORD replied, "Is it right for you
to be angry about this?"*

Jonah 4:1-4 (NLT)

Jonah was actually upset with God because Ninevah repented and would not be destroyed!

*Then Jonah went out to the east side of the city and made a shel-
ter to sit under as he waited to see if anything would happen to
the city. And the LORD God arranged for a leafy plant to grow
there, and soon it spread its broad leaves over Jonah's head,
shading him from the sun. This eased some of his discomfort,
and Jonah was very grateful for the plant.*

*But God also prepared a worm! The next morning at dawn the
worm ate through the stem of the plant, so that it soon died and
withered away. And as the sun grew hot, God sent a scorching
east wind to blow on Jonah. The sun beat down on his head until
he grew faint and wished to die.*

"Death is certainly better than this!" he exclaimed.

*Then God said to Jonah, "Is it right for you to be angry because
the plant died?" "Yes," Jonah retorted, "even angry enough
to die!" Then the LORD said, "You feel sorry about the plant,
though you did nothing to put it there. And a plant is only, at best,
short lived. But Nineveh has more than 120,000 people living in
spiritual darkness, not to mention all the animals. Shouldn't I
feel sorry for such a great city?"*

Jonah 4:5-11 (NLT)

Because Jonah is wallowing in self-pity, he refuses to rejoice
with thanksgiving that the Lord is merciful and compassionate and
has redeemed the city! He found more joy in the plant that God grew
for his relief from the hot sun than he did in the repentance of the
Ninevites. Where was Jonah's focus? On whom were his thoughts
centered? We can safely conclude that Jonah's thoughts were focused on himself. When Ninevah was spared, did he rejoice that

120,000 people had repented and were saved from destruction? No, he was angry that his prediction was not going to come to pass. He did not think these people deserved to be spared. In his own heart, he questioned the wisdom of God. God knew his heart and called Jonah to account for his reaction: "Is it right for you to be angry about this?"

♥ Heart Work
In what ways do you identify with Jonah?

What self-pitying thoughts do you struggle with? If you are having a hard time identifying them, consider that many of our self-pitying thoughts begin with words like: "I can't believe this happened to me!" "How could I be treated like this?"

Another great Bible hero, Elijah, also struggled with self-pity. After he slew the 350 prophets of Baal and called down fire from heaven, he became intimidated by a hot-tempered woman. He ran away and hid when he heard that there was a threat against his life:

Then he went on alone into the desert, traveling all day. He sat down under a solitary broom tree and prayed that he might die. "I have had enough, LORD," he said. "Take my life, for I am no better than my ancestors."

1 Kings 19:4 (NLT)

Elijah traveled 40 days into the desert until he reached Mt. Sinai, where he spent the night in a cave.

But the LORD said to him, "What are you doing here, Elijah?"

Two times God asked Elijah what he was doing in that cave and both times he gave the same response:

Elijah replied, "I have zealously served the LORD God Almighty. But the people of Israel have broken their covenant with you, torn down your altars, and killed every one of your prophets. I alone am left, and now they are trying to kill me, too."

1 Kings 19:10 (NLT)

It is probable that you, like Elijah, are not dealing with all the facts of your circumstances. Elijah did not see the entire picture of what God was accomplishing through him. Before time was established, God had planned how He was going to work out every circumstance. God gave Elijah his orders to appoint Hazael king of Syria, Jehu king of Israel, and Elisha as his own replacement. God informed Elijah that he was not alone in the offce of prophet; He told him there were 7,000 left in Israel who were faithful. Elijah then understood that God had not abandoned His throne, even though it appeared to him that all hope was lost!

So beloved, as we see in the case of these two men of God, self-pity can consume a person. You can get to the point where you think only about yourself, you lose perspective on the problem, and you want to escape the pain or die.

Those who pity themselves because of the circumstances in their lives fail to see God at work in them; they fail to see beyond what they perceive their need to be today. Those without self-pity, however, understand that God always has their best interests at heart, as well as His eternal purpose.

♥ Heart Work
How do these truths affect your thinking?

Have you failed to see God at work in your circumstances?

Do you believe God is at work even in difficult or frightening situations?

And we know that in all things God works for the good of those who love him, who have been called according to his purpose. For those God foreknew he also predestined to be conformed to the likeness of his Son, that he might be the firstborn among many brothers. Romans 8:28-29 (NIV)

81

The circumstances in your life are intended to change you for the better. Although it may not feel like it right now, God is using your woes and sorrows to reveal the contents of your heart and to help you in the transformation process.

Your circumstances are intentional and purposeful. Rather than view them from the negative, consider that God knows exactly what it will take to conform you to the image and likeness of Christ. He will bring just the right amount of pressure to bear on your heart to help you in the process of being changed into His image.

♥ *Heart Work*
What are some things you suspect God is working on in you through this time? Write out as many things as you can think of in your notebook.

Does seeing these areas of growth and change bring you encouragement? Why or why not?

Curing the Heart of Self-Pity

God's cure for self-pity is found in Psalm 37. In this Psalm, God counseled David—and counsels us—not to become discouraged as we see evil prosper. He reminds us that He is the Righteous One, the Judge and Jury over all the earth. Because we are His, we will triumph, but we must wait on Him and trust in His righteousness and justice. I would encourage you to do an in-depth study of Psalm 37.

You cannot depend on human reasoning or counsel to overcome any aspect of depression:

"I will destroy human wisdom and discard their most brilliant ideas." So where does this leave the philosophers, the scholars, and the world's brilliant debaters? God has made them all look foolish and has shown their wisdom to be useless nonsense.
1 Corinthians 1:19-20 (NLT)

"For My thoughts are not your thoughts, Nor are your ways My ways," says the LORD. "For as the heavens are higher than the earth, So are My ways higher than your ways, And My thoughts than your thoughts." Isaiah 55:8 (NIV)

Having hope to overcome is a result of understanding that all behaviors are the result of what we choose to believe and what we desire in our hearts. Self-pitying thoughts reflect a lack of gratitude to God and a lack of faith that God is sovereign over all of life.

What is the solution to self-pity? Begin to practice thankfulness. Rather than looking at how wrong and awful things are in your life, begin to ask, "What is God trying to tell me in this circumstance?" Each of life's trials has a purpose, a reason why God has allowed or, in some cases, brought the trial into your life. Each of these trials is tailor-made by your loving heavenly Father just for you! God knows exactly what it takes to get your attention, and what amount of pressure is necessary to change your heart. Trials are the refining fires of Christianity my friend.

♥ *Heart Work*
Do you practice gratitude? Are you a thankful person?

If your answer to the above questions was "no", write out what your natural response is.

Begin to look for opportunities to thank God for what is happening in your daily life. If this has not been your practice, you will be amazed as you begin to see just how actively God is working in your life. Looking at life from God's perspective is crucial in overcoming self-pity.

♥ *Heart Work*
Write out a list of things you have in your life to be thankful and grateful for. Be specific.

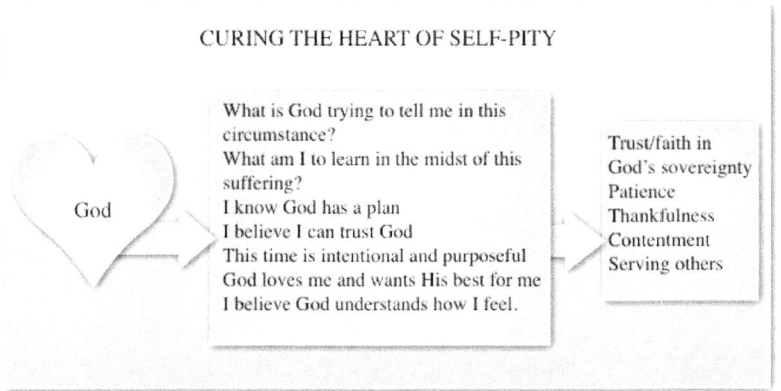

CURING THE HEART OF SELF-PITY

God

What is God trying to tell me in this circumstance?
What am I to learn in the midst of this suffering?
I know God has a plan
I believe I can trust God
This time is intentional and purposeful
God loves me and wants His best for me
I believe God understands how I feel.

Trust/faith in God's sovereignty
Patience
Thankfulness
Contentment
Serving others

When you begin to put on a heart of thankfulness and look at life from God's perspective, it is no longer what God is doing to you, but what God is doing through you in the lives of those around you.

I pray you now have a deepening understanding of this aspect of depression. I would suggest praying to our Lord a simple prayer of recognition of your own struggles with self-pity. You may want to pattern yours after this one:

Dear gracious heavenly Father, I confess to You that I struggle with the sin of self-pity. I admit that I often think only about the things that trouble me. At times I am so overwhelmed by them that I lose sight of Your faithfulness, goodness, and provision to assist me in any and every trouble I encounter in life. Lord, I confess to You that at times I do not believe that You are good or faithful, as is obvious by my speech and actions. Please help me, Lord, to understand Your sovereign plan for my life. Help me to accept hardships as refining fires that are conforming me to the image of your beloved Son, Jesus Christ. Thank You for my salvation Lord— something I truly don't deserve but possess through Your good grace toward me. Thank You for the forgiveness for my sin that comes through the shed blood of the Lord Jesus Christ. I ask Your help to overcome this dreadful sin habit, to put on an attitude of thanksgiving, and to trust in You. In Jesus' name, Amen.

Chapter 6
The Idolatrous Heart

The heart of idolatry is truly central to the issue of depression. Just like the other sins with which we struggle, it is rooted in the immaterial part of man we refer to as the heart. Remember that the heart contains your thoughts, beliefs, desires, mind, will, and emotions. This is why the heart can be referred to as the control center of your being. The heart of mankind is deceitful and wicked according to Jeremiah 17:9, and the sinful nature that we battle feeds the wicked desires of the heart.

> *When you follow the desires of your sinful nature, your lives will produce these evil results: sexual immorality, impure thoughts, eagerness for lustful pleasure, **idolatry,** participation in demonic activities, hostility, quarreling, jealousy, outbursts of anger, selfish ambition, divisions, the feeling that everyone is wrong except those in your own little group.*
>
> Galatians 5:19-20 (NLT, emphasis mine)

Friend, each of us struggles with the horrendous sin of idolatry on a daily basis, and we must realize we tend to minimize our sinful heart attitudes. As we read the words of Jesus and Paul, we can see that our biggest problem lies within our own hearts.

As Galatians 5 tells us, idolatry is a desire of our sinful nature. The idolatry of the heart is reflected in our choices, our words, our use of time, what or who we spend our money on, and where. We have been created to worship God, but our sinful lusts have driv-en us to worship and idolize other things; the things of the world.

Heart Work

Do you think that you have issues of idolatry?

In our culture, we tend to think of idolatry as an eastern religious system such as Buddhism or Hinduism, or as pagan worship of the trees and animals. But the truth is, idolatry is not only bowing down to statues, it is anything that means more to you than God does. It is manifested when getting what you want has become more important than what God desires for you. Simply put, anything that you love, desire or serve more than God is an idol of the heart. This is why a person who struggles with non-organic depression has a heart/soul problem, not a medical or psychological problem.

♥ *Heart Work*

Meditate on this statement for a few minutes: "The truth is, idolatry is not only bowing down to statues, it is anything that means more to you than God does."

Who or what means more to you than God does? You will know it when it has become more important to you than glorifying or obeying God. Write it in your journal.

We are constantly being tempted to sin in this manner. While many technological advances exist in the world, including new things to idolize and worship, Satan uses the same tricks and methods to bait the trap that he has employed since the Garden of Eden. We can look back to Genesis 3 to see them.

> *Now the serpent was the shrewdest of all the creatures the LORD God had made. "Really?" he asked the woman. "Did God really say you must not eat any of the fruit in the garden?"*
>
> Genesis 3:1 (NLT)

Satan planted doubt in the mind of the woman about what God had said.

> *"Of course we may eat it," the woman told him. "It's only the fruit from the tree at the center of the garden that we are not allowed to eat. God says we must not eat it or even touch it, or we will die."*
>
> *"You won't die!" the serpent hissed. "God knows that your eyes will be opened when you eat it. You will become just like God, knowing everything, both good and evil."*
>
> Genesis 3:3-4 (NLT)

The big lie occurs here, and the great temptation—"You will be like God." Man has wanted to be his own god since that time. Being your own god means freedom from accountability.

86

The woman was convinced. The fruit looked so fresh and delicious, and it would make her so wise! So she ate some of the fruit. She also gave some to her husband, who was with her. Then he ate it, too. At that moment, their eyes were opened, and they suddenly felt shame at their nakedness. So they strung fig leaves together around their hips to cover themselves.

Genesis 3:6-7 (NLT)

Thus they succumbed to the lust of the eyes, the lust of the flesh, and the pride of life. Sin and guilt entered the world, and to this day Satan uses the same tactics against us. We see this reiterated in John's first epistle to the churches:

For the world offers only the lust for physical pleasure, the lust for everything we see, and pride in our possessions. These are not from the Father. They are from this evil world.

1 John 2:16 (NLT)

Our idolatry takes many forms. Some people idolize money and possessions:

People who want to get rich fall into temptation and a trap and into many foolish and harmful desires that plunge men into ruin and destruction.

1 Timothy 6:9 (NIV)

Then he said to them, "Watch out! Be on your guard against all kinds of greed; a man's life does not consist in the abundance of his possessions."

Luke 12:15 (NIV)

Others idolize people such as celebrities, sports figures, and musicians. Look at the popularity of the program, "American Idol" and the millions of people who watch each week and vote for their "idol". Criminal rap artists are held in high esteem by the younger generation. The actions of high-priced athletes (who once were lauded for their abilities on the playing field but now are notorious for their antics off the field) are being emulated by high school players.

87

I have known mothers who idolize their children by building a child-centered home. These children grow up believing that they are the center of the world and expect others to cater to their every need and whim. When their felt needs that were catered to as children are not met as adults, they become depressed because the constant praise and adoration of the parents is no longer present. No one is telling them how good they are and puffng up their pride.

The bottom line is simple—we were born to worship. We have been created to worship God, but our sinful lusts have driven us to worship and idolize the things of the world.

♥ *Heart Work*
After reading the above section, can you see your own worship disorder?

Who or what are you worshipping? Money, fame, fitness/body, sex, material things (clothes, fashion, cars), job/career, children, spouse, marriage, independence, sports, food, etc.

Thank God that we have a High Priest who sympathizes with us in our weakness! After fasting for 40 days in the wilderness, Jesus Christ was presented by Satan with a choice to sin in idolatry:

> *Next the Devil took him to the peak of a very high mountain and showed him the nations of the world and all their glory. "I will give it all to you," he said, "if you will only kneel down and worship me." "Get out of here, Satan," Jesus told him. "For the Scriptures say, 'You must worship the Lord your God; serve only him.'"*

> Matthew 4:8-10 (NLT)

Serving only Him means that we deny our urge to idolize things and people. God made things available for you to enjoy and placed people in your life to love because this glorifies Him. You are not to worship or build your life around them, and those people and things certainly are not to replace your love for the Lord. As you may have already discovered, when your goals, dreams, and desires are in conflict with God's, you will experience sorrow. God's desire for you is to glorify Him, to live a life that honors and serves Him.

What you serve and obey is whatever you worship or place a high value on. God hates idolatry. Hundreds of verses in the Bible tell us of the hatred He has for those who worship anything or anyone other than Him.

Isaiah 44 gives an exposition of how foolish we can be and how easily we are led into idolatry. In this passage we find the woodsman who plants a tree and tends to it. God provides the rich soil and rain to nourish the tree, and the sun provides the light it needs to grow strong and tall. The woodsman cuts down the tree and uses part of it for firewood to roast the game God provides.

Then he takes what's left and makes his god: a carved idol! He falls down in front of it, worshiping and praying to it. "Rescue me," he says. "You are my god!"

Such stupidity and ignorance! Their eyes are closed, and they cannot see. Their minds are shut, and they cannot think. The person who made the idol never stops to reflect, "Why, it's just a block of wood! I burned half of it for heat and used it to bake my bread and roast my meat. How can the rest of it be a god? Should I bow down to worship a chunk of wood?" The poor, deluded fool feeds on ashes. He is trusting something that can give him no help at all. Yet he cannot bring himself to ask, "Is this thing, this idol that I'm holding in my hand, a lie?"

Isaiah 44:17-20 (NLT)

♥ *Heart Work*

Are the things and people you hold onto intended to rescue you, meet your needs, and make you feel better?

Are the things you worship really just ashes?

Are the things you worship going to save you from your felt needs?

Do you expect them to make you feel better, more secure, popular, loved?

Ask yourself whether what you are holding onto, this worship of self, is a lie.

Desires are not always wrong, but they can become idols if they come to mean more to you than living your life to glorify, worship, and serve God, and to minister to others. A good definition of idolatry is when you are willing to sin to get the object of your desire.

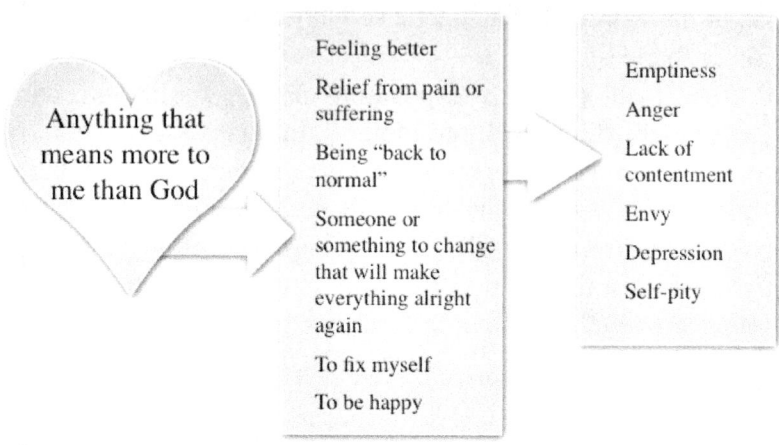

♥ Heart Work
Have you been willing to sin to get relief from pain, to be happy, or to attain any of the other feelings mentioned above?

If having your felt needs met has become so important to you that you are willing to violate God's Word to have them, then you have crossed the line from desire to worship.

The one thing the depressed person idolizes above all else is self. That's right. If you are depressed, the one person who means the most to you in the world is you. How can I say that?

People who are depressed typically have their whole focus on the desire to feel better. Feeling better is the focus of every day, and it becomes the goal of every day, the recurring thought, the overwhelming driving force. This desire is so self-focused that it leaves no room for you to see what God may be accomplishing in you and through you during this time. The focus on self leaves no room for worship of God. This self-focused desire is fed by ads in magazines, on billboards, and on television that lead you to believe it is not okay to feel sad, unhappy, or "bad".

♥ Heart Work
Have you made the focus of your life "feeling better"? You may have to think about that before answering. Use The Idolatrous Heart Diagram to help you come to a conclusion. Write your thoughts in your notebook.

When the depression does not lift despite your pleadings with God, the focus on self becomes even more intense. You begin to question the goodness of God, the righteousness of God, and the sovereignty of God.

The Lord often uses internal pain to alert us to something that He wants to change in our hearts. We must not run from the pain. James says,

> *Whenever trouble comes your way, let it be an opportunity for joy. For when your faith is tested, your endurance has a chance to grow. So let it grow, for when your endurance is fully developed, you will be strong in character and ready for anything.*
>
> James 1:2-4 (NLT)

Correcting the Idolatrous Heart

> *And we are instructed to turn from godless living and sinful pleasures. We should live in this evil world with self-control, right conduct, and devotion to God, while we look forward to that wonderful event when the glory of our great God and Savior, Jesus Christ, will be revealed.*
>
> Titus 2:12-13 (NLT)

> *Therefore, my beloved, flee from idolatry.*
>
> 1 Corinthians 10:14 (NKJV)

> *Dear children, keep away from anything that might take God's place in your hearts.*
>
> 1 John 5:21 (NLT)

It may be diffcult for you to see yourself as a person who has idols of the heart. We simply don't think that way unless the Word of God penetrates our self-deception and the Holy Spirit reveals it to us. Friend, I have presented a good case for why a depressed person may fit in the category of an idolater; I would urge you to go to God right now and ask Him to reveal to you if indeed you are one who struggles with this sin.

You might want to pray a prayer similar to this one:

Dear Lord God, I am struggling so much with wanting to feel better and to have these depressive moods lift from me so I can go on living as before. I am learning that this may not be Your will for me, that my desires to feel better may have become idolatry. I ask you, Lord, to reveal to me through Your Word if this is so. Please, Holy Spirit, take the Word of God and apply it to my heart as you did for King David. If I am guilty, Lord, my desire is to repent of my sin and turn toward worshiping and serving You only from this moment forward. When I am tempted to revert back to my former thoughts and become self-focused again, remind me of my commitment.
You are a mighty and powerful God. I love you and thank You for Your forgiveness through the sacrifice of Your Son, Christ Jesus. In His name I pray, Amen.

If this is truly your desire, your prayer must be accompanied by actions that will demonstrate the fruit of your repentance.

♥ *Heart Work*

Begin to admit that the sin of idolatry exists in your heart. If you prayed the above prayer, you began to admit this, but it is an ongoing process. If you have struggled with idolatry for a long time, you have habits that are deeply engrained. You will find yourself admitting and confessing this sin frequently, but do not be further discouraged!

Recognize that God is cleaning out the deception in your heart.

Identify exactly what you want that you are not getting, and write it out in your notebook. Some examples would be feeling better or having a better day.

Identify if your desire is biblical, and support it with Scripture (in context). This is important because emotions can lead us to justify our desire for certain things.

Feelings prove unreliable as a method of living life to glorify God.

And so, dear brothers and sisters, I plead with you to give your bodies to God. Let them be a living and holy sacrifice—the kind he will accept. When you think of what he has done for you,

92

is this too much to ask? Don't copy the behavior and customs of this world, but let God transform you into a new person by changing the way you think. Then you will know what God wants you to do, and you will know how good and pleasing and perfect his will really is.

Romans 12:1-2 (NLT)

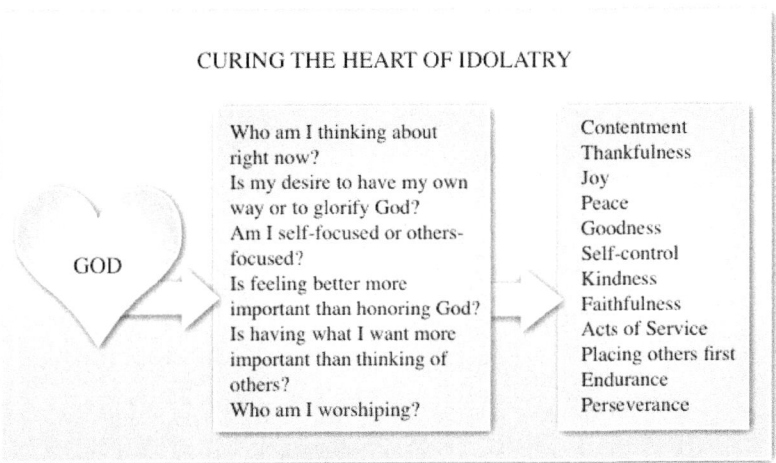

CURING THE HEART OF IDOLATRY

God wants to change the way you think, which will change the way you live. Reject the thoughts of what you want and desire for each day. Begin to get up and go about life as though you had what you want. Begin to obey God by fulfilling your responsibilities to your family, church, job, or friends.

You will find more on how to correct these sinful patterns in the next section. For now, I want you to see that a big part of your thinking is rooted in sinful indulgence.

Chapter 7
The Sinfully Indulgent Heart

The heart that indulges is closely related to the heart of idolatry. Consider a person who is habitually irresponsible. He lives his life by his feelings. For example, he doesn't usually feel like working, so he chooses relaxation, video games, television. If he is a student, his homework is poorly done, and when it comes to manual labor or chores, he makes a half-hearted effort at best. He is a miserable guy who finds himself always expecting someone to get on his case for a job poorly done. He lives his life looking over his shoulder. This causes him to be irritable, angry, and resentful of those who would hold him accountable for his actions or lack thereof.

Now consider a person who has been told she is depressed. She also is living her life by how she feels. If she feels like crying, she can spend the whole day doing it. If she feels like sleeping, she will avoid her responsibilities and stay in bed all day, or she'll doze off in front of the television or a movie. She too is waiting for someone to get on her case for jobs not done. She is irritable, angry, and resentful of those who would hold her accountable for her actions or lack of actions. If you question her behavior, she cries out that you don't understand! She insists that she has an illness and can't help herself.

In both cases, the hearts of these individuals are turned toward self-indulgence. If they don't feel like it, they don't do it! That is why self-indulgence is so closely related to idolatry, because it is idolatry! It is idolizing what you do or don't want, what you feel or don't feel, and making that into the god you serve and obey!

THE HEART OF SINFUL INDULGENCE

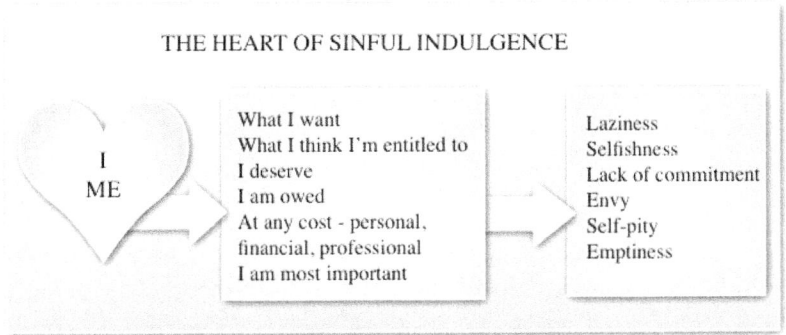

I
ME

What I want
What I think I'm entitled to
I deserve
I am owed
At any cost - personal,
financial, professional
I am most important

Laziness
Selfishness
Lack of commitment
Envy
Self-pity
Emptiness

Make it your ambition to lead a quiet life, to mind your own business and to work with your hands, just as we told you, so that your daily life may win the respect of outsiders and so that you will not be dependent on anybody.

1 Thessalonians 4:11-12 (NIV)

Take a lesson from the ants, you lazybones. Learn from their ways and be wise! Even though they have no prince, governor, or ruler to make them work, they labor hard all summer, gathering food for the winter. But you, lazybones, how long will you sleep? When will you wake up? I want you to learn this lesson: A little extra sleep, a little more slumber, a little folding of the hands to rest—and poverty will pounce on you like a bandit; scarcity will attack you like an armed robber.

Proverbs 6:6-11 (NLT)

Someone with a heart of sinful indulgence lacks discipline in most areas of life. He tends to drink too much, eat too much, and seeks pleasure in all areas of life. This can lead to drunkenness, sexual immorality, and wrong living.

♥ *Heart Work*

In your notebook, write the ways you indulge yourself.

Not every indulgence is sinful! Indulging in a piece of cake or a bowl of ice cream is not sinful for most of us. Neither (under most conditions) is buying something you want or taking a nap. However, there is a point at which even good things can become sinful.

Are there things you indulge in that have become stumbling blocks for you? Write them in your notebook, then write how you know that they have become sinful indulgences.

Place your desires and wants on the altar of sacrifice to God.

Then he said to them, "Watch out! Be on your guard against all kinds of greed; a man's life does not consist in the abundance of his possessions."

Luke 12:15 (NIV)

But people who long to be rich fall into temptation and are trapped by many foolish and harmful desires that plunge them into ruin and destruction.

1 Timothy 6:9 (NLT)

♥*Heart Work*
Prior to reading this section, did you think of your indulgences as sinful or greedy?

Have you changed your mind? If so, what caused the change?

Correcting the Heart of Idolatry and Sinful Indulgence

The more you begin to prayerfully desire to include the "one another's" in your life, the less your focus will be on indulging yourself.

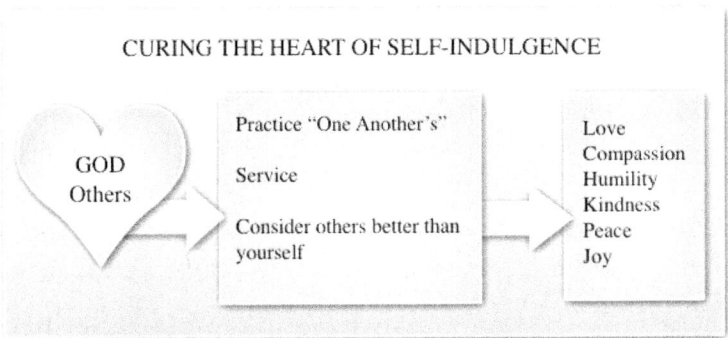

CURING THE HEART OF SELF-INDULGENCE

A person with a heart of sinful indulgence must begin to consider and act on the "one another's" of Scripture. Read the following list of New Testament verses, all taken from the New King James Version:

The "One Another's" of Scripture

Salt is good, but if the salt loses its flavor, how will you season it? Have salt in yourselves, and have peace with one another.

Mark 9:50

A new commandment I give to you, that you love one another; as I have loved you, that you also love one another. By this all will know that you are My disciples, if you have love for one another.

John 13:34-35

This is My commandment, that you love one another as I have loved you.

John 15:12

These things I command you, that you love one another.

John 15:17

So we, being many, are one body in Christ, and individually members of one another.

Romans 12:5

Be kindly affectionate to one another with brotherly love, in honor giving preference to one another.

Romans 12:10

Be of the same mind toward one another. Do not set your mind on high things, but associate with the humble. Do not be wise in your own opinion.

Romans 12:16

Owe no one anything except to love one another, for he who loves another has fulfilled the law.

Romans 13:8

Therefore let us not judge one another anymore, but rather resolve this, not to put a stumbling block or a cause to fall in our brother's way.

Romans 14:13

Now may the God of patience and comfort grant you to be like-minded toward one another, according to Christ Jesus.

Romans 15:5

Therefore receive one another, just as Christ also received us, to the glory of God.

Romans 15:7

Now I myself am confident concerning you, my brethren, that you also are full of goodness, filled with all knowledge, able also to admonish one another.

Romans 15:14

Greet one another with a holy kiss. The churches of Christ greet you.

Romans 16:16

Now therefore, it is already an utter failure for you that you go to law against one another. Why do you not rather accept wrong? Why do you not rather let yourselves be cheated?

1 Corinthians 6:7

Do not deprive one another except with consent for a time, that you may give yourselves to fasting and prayer; and come together again so that Satan does not tempt you because of your lack of self-control.

1 Corinthians 7:5

Therefore, my brethren, when you come together to eat, wait for one another.

1 Corinthians 11:33

That there should be no schism in the body, but that the members should have the same care for one another.

1 Corinthians 12:25

All the brethren greet you. Greet one another with a holy kiss.

1 Corinthians 16:20

Greet one another with a holy kiss.

2 Corinthians 13:12

For you, brethren, have been called to liberty; only do not use liberty as an opportunity for the flesh, but through love serve one another. For all the law is fulfilled in one word, even in this: "You shall love your neighbor as yourself." But if you bite and devour one another, beware lest you be consumed by one another!

Galatians 5:13-15

Let us not become conceited, provoking one another, envying one another.

Galatians 5:26

I, therefore, the prisoner of the Lord, beseech you to walk worthy of the calling with which you were called, with all lowliness and gentleness, with longsuffering, bearing with one another in love, endeavoring to keep the unity of the Spirit in the bond of peace.

Ephesians 4:1-3

Therefore, putting away lying, "Let each one of you speak truth with his neighbor," for we are members of one another.

Ephesians 4:25

And be kind to one another, tenderhearted, forgiving one another, even as God in Christ forgave you.

Ephesians 4:32

Speaking to one another in psalms and hymns and spiritual songs, singing and making melody in your heart to the Lord.

Ephesians 5:19

...submitting to one another in the fear of God.

Ephesians 5:21

Do not lie to one another, since you have put off the old man with his deeds.

Colossians 3:9

Therefore, as the elect of God, holy and beloved, put on tender mercies, kindness, humility, meekness, longsuffering; bearing with one another, and forgiving one another, if anyone has a complaint against another; even as Christ forgave you, so you also must do.

Colossians 3:12-13

Let the word of Christ dwell in you richly in all wisdom, teaching and admonishing one another in psalms and hymns and spiritual songs, singing with grace in your hearts to the Lord.

Colossians 3:16

And may the Lord make you increase and abound in love to one and to all, just as we do to you.

1 Thessalonians 3:12

But concerning brotherly love you have no need that I should write to you, for you yourselves are taught by God to love one another.

1 Thessalonians 4:9

Therefore comfort one another with these words.

1 Thessalonians 4:18

Therefore comfort each other and edify one another, just as you also are doing.

1 Thessalonians 5:11

But exhort one another daily, while it is called "Today," lest any of you be hardened through the deceitfulness of sin.

Hebrews 3:13

And let us consider one another in order to stir up love and good works.

Hebrews 10:24

...not forsaking the assembling of ourselves together, as is the manner of some, but exhorting one another, and so much the more as you see the Day approaching.

Hebrews 10:25

Do not speak evil of one another, brethren. He who speaks evil of a brother and judges his brother, speaks evil of the law and judges the law. But if you judge the law, you are not a doer of the law but a judge.

James 4:11

Do not grumble against one another, brethren, lest you be condemned. Behold, the Judge is standing at the door!

James 5:9

Confess your trespasses to one another, and pray for one another, that you may be healed. The effective, fervent prayer of a righteous man avails much.

James 5:16

Since you have purified your souls in obeying the truth through the Spirit in sincere love of the brethren, love one another fervently with a pure heart.

1 Peter 1:22

Finally, all of you be of one mind, having compassion for one another; love as brothers, be tenderhearted, be courteous.

1 Peter 3:8

And above all things have fervent love for one another, for "love will cover a multitude of sins." Be hospitable to one another without grumbling. As each one has received a gift, minister it to one another, as good stewards of the manifold grace of God.

1 Peter 4:8-10

Likewise you younger people, submit yourselves to your elders. Yes, all of you be submissive to one another, and be clothed with humility, for "God resists the proud, But gives grace to the humble."

1 Peter 5:5

Greet one another with a kiss of love. Peace to you all who are in Christ Jesus. Amen.

1 Peter 5:14

But if we walk in the light as He is in the light, we have fellowship with one another, and the blood of Jesus Christ His Son cleanses us from all sin.

1 John 1:7

For this is the message that you heard from the beginning, that we should love one another...

1 John 3:11

And this is His commandment: that we should believe on the name of His Son Jesus Christ and love one another, as He gave us commandment.

1 John 3:23

Beloved, let us love one another, for love is of God; and everyone who loves is born of God and knows God.

1 John 4:7

You might want to begin with a prayer similar to this one:

Dear precious Heavenly Father, after looking at the list of "one another's," I see now why I struggle so much with sinful indulgence. My focus has been all on myself, and I have not desired to serve or love other people as much as I have served and loved myself. I confess to you my sin of selfishness and sinful indulgence. I am sorry that I have ignored the needs of my fellow man, and I ask Your help in putting others before myself. Remind me to consider others, Lord, when I am tempted to return to my sinful and selfish ways. Thank You for being faithful to answer my prayer and plea for help in this area of my life. In Jesus' name, Amen.

Now that you have committed to a course of action in prayer, it is time to get down to the hard work of serving others. There are innumerable places to begin serving others, but I suggest you begin with those in your home and family. These are the people you have hurt the most by your indulgences. Begin small or big, just begin! I am sure you just need to look around you to notice many ways you can begin to serve. Pick up dishes, fold a load of laundry, wash the car, or prepare a meal for an elderly person. At church you can offer to work in the church nursery, collect the Sunday offerings, work at the help desk on Sunday mornings, or plant yourself at the door with a warm smile and cheery greeting to those who enter. If you have the availability to volunteer, you are especially blessed. Nursing homes love people who are willing to come and spend time with the residents, assisting with games and crafts, playing music for them, or just being a new face to share a kind word with them. The opportunities are endless!

I have seen improvement in my counselees who follow through on serving others. When your focus is on someone else, you will quickly find relief from the feelings of depression. It is not acceptable to wait until you feel better to begin to serve. You must begin to serve first, and then you will feel better. Obedience to the Word of God will bring joy to your heart that nothing else can. You were made to serve God and others, so the sooner you get about God's business the better!

Beloved, if God so loved us, we also ought to love one another. No one has seen God at any time. If we love one another, God abides in us, and His love has been perfected in us.

1 John 4:11-12 (NKJV)

And now I plead with you, lady, not as though I wrote a new commandment to you, but that which we have had from the beginning: that we love one another.

2 John 5 (NKJV)

104

♥Heart Work

Go back over the list of "One Another's" and mark or highlight those that you know are problematic for you. Perhaps you realize that you are not obedient in some area, and didn't see its importance before reading this section, but mark them anyway.

Then, choose one or two of your highlighted verses and determine exactly how you can begin to include them in your life every day, at least once.
Go out of your way to make them happen!
Thinking of others, when you are used to being self-focused, requires a plan and intentionality to implement it. Write out your plan in your notebook.

Chapter 8
The Heart that Lacks Assurance

The heart that lacks assurance is either within a person who is unsaved or within a person who professes to be a Christian, but is acting carnally. A person who is unsure of his or her eternal destiny or salvation is unsettled inside. There may be an uneasiness or fear of almost everything. People who doubt their salvation have no idea who they really are. They often spend their entire lives "searching for themselves". The Bible is clear about the condition of people who are unsaved, meaning they have not accepted Jesus Christ as their Lord and Savior.

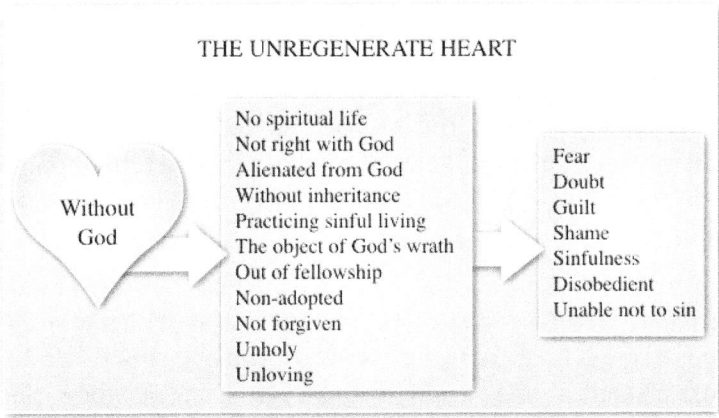

THE UNREGENERATE HEART

Without God

No spiritual life
Not right with God
Alienated from God
Without inheritance
Practicing sinful living
The object of God's wrath
Out of fellowship
Non-adopted
Not forgiven
Unholy
Unloving

Fear
Doubt
Guilt
Shame
Sinfulness
Disobedient
Unable not to sin

If you are a believer, you may lack assurance because of a specific sin you have committed in the past or because you struggle in overcoming sinful patterns of living. I have counseled many women who carry the guilt of abortion, for example, who are not sure whether God has forgiven them. I have also counseled those who have a persistent pattern of life dominating sin that causes them to question their salvation.

♥ *Heart Work*
Do you find that you are unsure about where you stand with God?
Are you fearful that God doesn't love you?
If so, is it because of something you have done in the past?
Is it because you feel you don't measure up, aren't good enough, or struggle with sin?

It is possible you are living your life right now as an unbeliever would, living for yourself or living for the pleasures of life rather than the glory of God. This has been called living as a carnal Christian and will cause you to lack assurance of your salvation.

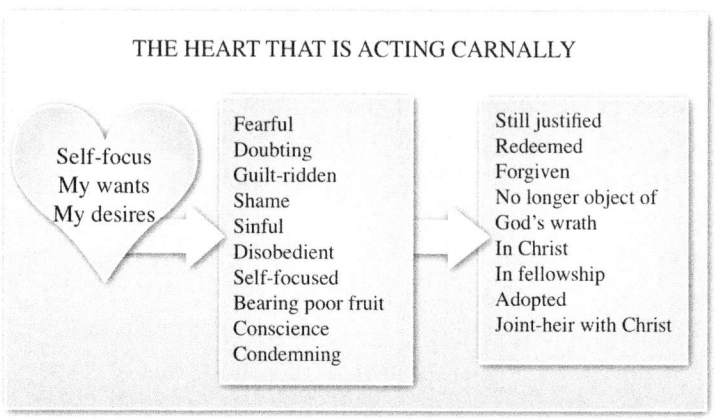

THE HEART THAT IS ACTING CARNALLY

Self-focus
My wants
My desires

Fearful
Doubting
Guilt-ridden
Shame
Sinful
Disobedient
Self-focused
Bearing poor fruit
Conscience
Condemning

Still justified
Redeemed
Forgiven
No longer object of
God's wrath
In Christ
In fellowship
Adopted
Joint-heir with Christ

A person whose life is characterized by sinful words and deeds has good reason to be uneasy about their spiritual condition. Because of improper presentation of the gospel, we have churches full of unconverted people all trying to work out a salvation they do not even possess.

Many people base their salvation on a past event such as praying a prayer, walking an aisle or raising their hand when they are asked if they want to "receive Jesus as their Savior". Sadly, many of those who have embraced a prayer have no clue as to what was supposed to happen, or what supposedly did happen to them in that moment.

How will you know if you are a believer in Christ who has been genuinely converted and who understands the saving grace of Jesus Christ?

We have churches full of people who are confused because their lives have not changed one bit since they have prayed that prayer or asked Jesus into their heart. They have no new desires, no new direction, and they cannot understand why "God does not work for me". They are defeated and miserable, waiting for this joy and jubilation they see in others at church.

Praying a prayer, asking Jesus into your heart, and walking an aisle are not true evidences of salvation. It is more important to know how your life has changed since you asked Jesus into your heart, prayed that prayer, or surrendered your life.

Many, many Christians wonder from time to time if they are truly regenerate, but that question should not be a daily part of your life. If you truly doubt your salvation, it may be that God is using this season of depression to bring you to this point of decision in your life—as a tool to reveal that you are in need of a Savior.

♥ *Heart Work*
How has your life changed since you became a Christian?
Is there enough evidence to convict you of being a Christian?
Where is God in your trial?
     Does He stand far off?
     Is He not involved?
     Do you think He cares?
Do you secretly wonder if you're a Christian?

If you have been a Christian or have been around a Bible-believing church for any time at all, you have heard the Gospel, and this may be completely familiar to you. I would like to take the next few minutes and address those who do not at this time share a relationship with our heavenly Father.

The first thing you must accept and understand is that the Bible is the only source we have to help us understand who we really are. From the Creator of man, we have the facts about man, which are far superior to any psychological theory about man. The Bible gives us specific facts about what is normal, what is abnormal, and how to change.

If you do not believe that the Bible is the actual Word of God, I would urge you to reconsider your opinion! I cannot commit much space in this writing to addressing the accuracy of the Scriptures, but I would urge you to get a copy of the Bible for yourself and begin to read it. Many books are available to assist you in understanding what the Bible says about itself:

All Scripture is inspired by God and is useful to teach us what is true and to make us realize what is wrong in our lives. It straightens us out and teaches us to do what is right. It is God's way of preparing us in every way, fully equipped for every good thing God wants us to do.

2 Timothy 3:16-17 (NLT)

The superior answers of the Bible lead us to understand that we can have victory over diffcult events of the past and present. It describes issues and problems of life that are far deeper than feelings.

The Bible has the answers to help people. It has the answer to the deepest issue of your life—your personal relationship with Jesus Christ. This relationship is foundational to victory over depression and other problems of life. Look at what the apostle John wrote in his first letter about Jesus and how He affects our lives:

The one who existed from the beginning is the one we have heard and seen. We saw him with our own eyes and touched him with our own hands. He is Jesus Christ, the Word of life. This one who is life from God was shown to us, and we have seen him. And now we testify and announce to you that he is the one who is eternal life. He was with the Father, and then he was shown to us. We are telling you about what we ourselves have actually seen and heard, so that you may have fellowship with us. And our fellowship is with the Father and with his Son, Jesus Christ. We are writing these things so that our joy will be complete.

This is the message he has given us to announce to you: God is light and there is no darkness in him at all. So we are lying if we say we have fellowship with God but go on living in spiritual darkness. We are not living in the truth. But if we are living in the light of God's presence, just as Christ is, then we have fellowship with each other, and the blood of Jesus, his Son, cleanses us from every sin.

If we say we have no sin, we are only fooling ourselves and refusing to accept the truth. But if we confess our sins to him, he is faithful and just to forgive us and to cleanse us from every wrong. 1 John 1:1-9 (NLT)

These are powerful words! Clearly you are either in the light or in the darkness. Without the power of God through Jesus Christ, you are in the darkness. If you are in spiritual darkness, it is impossible to achieve real change in your life. This is because without Christ we are sinful and incredibly wicked. The Bible says that our sin separates us from a holy, sinless God:

For all have sinned; all fall short of God's glorious standard.
Romans 3:23 (NLT)

It isn't just the sin you commit each day that causes you to fall short; the truth is that you were born a sinner.

♥*Heart Work*
Deep down, do you think you are a sinner?

Do you think you are a pretty good person who makes mistakes?

How do the above Scriptures affect you? Do they bring unease? Confidence? Anger? Self-righteousness? Fear? Write about it in your notebook.

You will be proved right in what you say, and your judgment against me is just. For I was born a sinner—yes, from the moment my mother conceived me. But you desire honesty from the heart, so you can teach me to be wise in my inmost being. Purify me from my sins and I will be clean, wash me, and I will be whiter than snow.
Psalm 51:1-7 (NLT)

Because of sin, there will be judgment. The psalmist David asked for pardon from his sins; for redemption; for salvation. The Bible makes it clear that because of their sin, unsaved people will not inherit the kingdom of God:

Do you not know that the wicked will not inherit the kingdom of God? Do not be deceived: Neither the sexually immoral nor idolaters nor adulterers nor male prostitutes nor homosexual offenders nor thieves nor the greedy nor drunkards nor slanderers nor swindlers will inherit the kingdom of God.
1 Corinthians 6:9-10 (NIV)

But the cowardly, the unbelieving, the vile, the murderers, the sexually immoral, those who practice magic arts, the idolaters and all liars—their place will be in the fiery lake of burning sulfur. This is the second death.

Revelation 21:8 (NIV)

To not "inherit the kingdom of God" means that you will be eternally separated from Him. When you take your last breath, you will be lost and without hope for all eternity. You will have no second chances and no reprieve from suffering.

Perhaps you have heard this before and discounted it. I would urge you not to harden your heart today. Paul said in this passage of Romans:

But no, you won't listen. So you are storing up terrible punishment for yourself because of your stubbornness in refusing to turn from your sin. For there is going to come a day of judgment when God, the just judge of all the world, will judge all people according to what they have done. He will give eternal life to those who persist in doing what is good, seeking after the glory and honor and immortality that God offers. But he will pour out his anger and wrath on those who live for themselves, who refuse to obey the truth and practice evil deeds.

Romans 2:5-8 (NLT)

For the wages of sin is death, but the gift of God is eternal life in Christ Jesus our Lord.

Romans 6:23 (NIV)

♥ *Heart Work*
Now that you've read a little more of what the Lord says about who you really are apart from Christ, have your thoughts changed at all?

The judgment to come may be terrible and terrifying news for you to read. If it were the end of the story, I would agree! But God is gracious toward us, and did not leave us in this state.

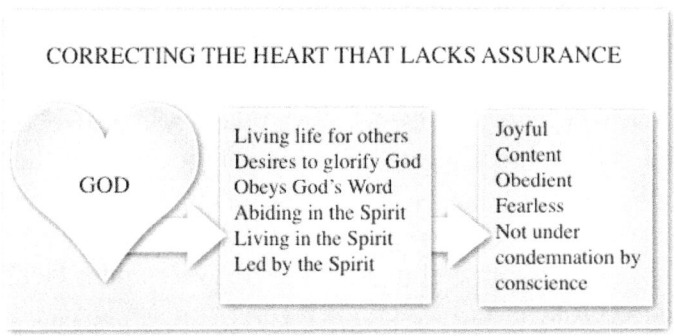

CORRECTING THE HEART THAT LACKS ASSURANCE

| GOD | Living life for others
Desires to glorify God
Obeys God's Word
Abiding in the Spirit
Living in the Spirit
Led by the Spirit | Joyful
Content
Obedient
Fearless
Not under
condemnation by
conscience |

The good news is that Jesus Christ came to redeem sinners and to set us free from the penalty of sin and death.

But God showed his great love for us by sending Christ to die for us while we were still sinners. And since we have been made right in God's sight by the blood of Christ, he will certainly save us from God's judgment.

Romans 5:8-9 (NLT)

God has provided a way for you to be made right with Him through Jesus Christ.

For God made Christ, who never sinned, to be the offering for our sin, so that we could be made right with God through Christ.

1 Corinthians 5:21 (NLT)

The only way to be made right with God is through Jesus Christ. You must understand and believe that there is nothing you can do to save yourself.

The sinful mind is hostile to God. It does not submit to God's law, nor can it do so. Those controlled by the sinful nature cannot please God.

Romans 8:7-8 (NIV)

Without Christ, it is Impossible to Submit to God or Obey Him.

Once you were dead, doomed forever because of your many sins. You used to live just like the rest of the world, full of sin, obeying Satan, the mighty prince of the power of the air. He is the spirit at work in the hearts of those who refuse to obey God. All of us used to live that way, following the passions and desires of our evil nature. We were born with an evil nature, and we were under God's anger just like everyone else.

♥ Heart Work

Have you believed that you could be a good person and go to heaven when you die?

Have you tried to live sacrificially and be kind, thinking that would gain you entrance into heaven?

Do you believe your good works earn you special favor with God?

But God is so rich in mercy, and he loved us so very much, that even while we were dead because of our sins, he gave us life when he raised Christ from the dead. (It is only by God's special favor [grace] that you have been saved!)

Ephesians 2:1-5 (NLT)

God saved you by his special favor (grace) when you believed. You can't take credit for this; it is a gift from God. Salvation is not a reward for the good things we have done, so none of us can boast about it.

Ephesians 2:8-9 (NLT)

He saved us, not because of the good things we did, but because of his mercy. He washed away our sins and gave us a new life through the Holy Spirit. He generously poured out the Spirit upon us because of what Jesus Christ our Savior did. He declared us not guilty (justification) because of his great kindness. And now we know that we will inherit eternal life.

Titus 3:5-7 (NLT, parenthesis mine)

Salvation is a gift of God that we receive by faith. You must believe that you are a sinner in need of salvation, and that you have no way to save yourself from the penalty of your sin. Instead, believe that Jesus Christ came to pay the penalty for your sin by giving His life for you on the cross.

Do you see your need for the Savior? There is no special formula to receive Christ—just an understanding that you are a sinner in need of Salvation, which is a gift of God that we receive by faith. You must believe you are a sinner in need of salvation; you have no way to save yourself from the penalty of your sin. Instead, believe that Jesus Christ came to pay the penalty for your sin by giving His life for you on the cross.

For Christ died for sins once for all, the righteous for the unrighteous, to bring you to God. He was put to death in the body but made alive by the Spirit.

1 Peter 3:18 (NIV)

♥ *Heart Work*
This is a deeply personal decision. No one can make it for you, and you can't get saved on the coattails of someone else. Your parents' faith won't save you; attending church won't save you; being a good person won't save you either. If you have any doubt about your eternal destiny and your spiritual condition, there is a reason for that doubt!

Reading this book and journaling your answers to the questions will not be as helpful as spending time with the Lord, searching your soul, and reading what His Word says regarding salvation.

For if you confess with your mouth that Jesus is Lord and believe in your heart that God raised him from the dead, you will be saved. For it is by believing in your heart that you are made right with God, and it is by confessing with your mouth that you are saved. As the Scriptures tell us, "Anyone who believes in him will not be disappointed." Jew and Gentile are the same in this respect. They all have the same Lord, who generously gives his riches to all who ask for them. For "Anyone who calls on the name of the Lord will be saved."

Romans 10:9-13 (NLT)

If it is your desire to call upon the name of the Lord and be saved, you can receive Him right where you are. No magic dust, or formula, or special prayer. God sees your heart, and what He asks is that you speak to Him in your own words, confessing your belief in Jesus Christ as Lord, your understanding of what He accomplished in His death on the cross, and your personal need for Him to cleanse you from your sin. Ask Him to be your Savior.

The prayer that follows has no "magic words"; it is simply intended to give you a place to start talking to God, because I know some people really struggle with knowing what to say. The words should ultimately be your own. The most important thing is that you mean what you are saying as you pray.

Dear God,
I never understood before the desperate condition I have been in. Maybe You tried to tell me before and I was unwilling to listen. Dear God, I am so sorry for rejecting You up to this point in my life. I have been stubborn and rebellious toward You. I know now that I am a sinner and that there is nothing—no works—that I can do to bridge the gap between You and me. I also understand that Jesus Christ paid the penalty for my sin on the cross, and that by doing so He made a way for me to be reconciled to You. I would like to ask You, God, to forgive me for all my sin—past, present, and future—through the shed blood of the Lord Jesus Christ, and to give to me the Person of the Holy Spirit to indwell me from this moment forward. I trust by faith that by confessing with my mouth that Jesus Christ is Lord, and believing in my heart that He was raised from the dead, I am now in a right relationship with You and can call You my heavenly Father. Thank You for saving me from my sins. In Jesus' name I pray. Amen.

♥*Heart Work*
If you have fallen on His grace and confessed you need the Savior, confessed your sin, and asked Him to redeem and adopt you as His own child, He is faithful to do it. He graciously washes you clean and places His Holy Spirit within you.

Therefore, since we have been made right in God's sight by faith, we have peace with God because of what Jesus Christ our Lord has done for us.

Romans 5:1 (NLT)

But you were washed, you were sanctified, you were justified in the name of the Lord Jesus Christ and by the Spirit of our God.

1 Corinthians 6:11

As a believer, you have the ability to learn and apply biblical principles that will help deal with depression. When you understand that you are a child of God and part of His family (John 1:12, Romans 8:16), you have a different response to trouble. You have as your ally the God of the universe, and nothing is impossible for Him. When you understand that you are a new creation in Christ (2 Corinthians 5:17), you do not need to be burdened with guilt for the sins of the past.

Once a person is a child of God, he or she has access to God.

For through him (Jesus Christ) we both have access to the Father by one Spirit.

Ephesians 2:18 (NIV)

Once a person is a child of God, he or she has hope!

But when the kindness and love of God our Savior appeared, he saved us, not because of righteous things we had done, but because of his mercy. He saved us through the washing of rebirth and renewal by the Holy Spirit, whom he poured out on us generously through Jesus Christ our Savior, so that, having been justified by his grace, we might become heirs having the hope of eternal life.

Titus 3:4-:7 (NIV)

Your hope is certain. It is not a pie-in-the-sky-it-might-happen kind of thing! The hope of a believer in the forgiveness of Jesus Christ is rock solid and irrevocable! A very wise pastor once reminded his congregation, "We can't lose by our actions what we did not gain by our actions!" In other words, if there was nothing I could do to gain Christ, then there is nothing I can do to lose Him either. No sin can separate us from His love!

♥ Heart Work

Are you convinced that God loves you?

Those who have a very sinful past express concern that God would never want someone like them. They wrongly believe that God doesn't want them because they aren't clean enough! Have you ever had those thoughts? Write about them in your notebook right now.

Do you think that there is anything that you can do to change God's love for you?

> And I am convinced that nothing can ever separate us from his love. Death can't, and life can't. The angels can't, and the demons can't. Our fears for today, our worries about tomorrow, and even the powers of hell can't keep God's love away. Whether we are high above the sky or in the deepest ocean, nothing in all creation will ever be able to separate us from the love of God that is revealed in Christ Jesus our Lord.
>
> Romans 8:38-39 (NLT)

What truths are contained in Romans 8:38-39? Write them out in your notebook.

What does this mean for you?

My hope for you is that you have found the assurance you have been looking for, either as a new believer, or as one who needed to be reminded of your unshakable position in Christ.

Chapter 9
The Guilty Heart

Guilt is a major contributor to depression. It is important to determine if the guilt is true or false.

Distinguishing Between True & False Guilt

I believe that the only person who is truly guilty before God is the one who is unsaved. This is a positional guilt. As you read in the previous section on assurance, unbelievers are truly guilty before God for all their sin. Their guilt is real and their feelings of guilt are real. Sometimes, God uses feelings of guilt to bring someone to Christ. In every situation, guilt helps us realize that something is out of order.

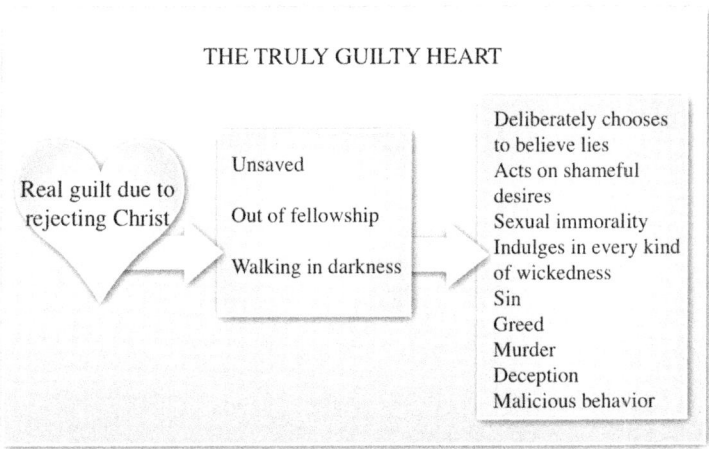

THE TRULY GUILTY HEART

Real guilt due to rejecting Christ

Unsaved

Out of fellowship

Walking in darkness

Deliberately chooses to believe lies
Acts on shameful desires
Sexual immorality
Indulges in every kind of wickedness
Sin
Greed
Murder
Deception
Malicious behavior

The feelings of guilt in unregenerate people are valid and come from a sense of God's divine judgment. They are culpable for their sin. They are under God's wrath and subject to His divine and righteous judgment. The experience and feelings of guilt are intended to move a person toward reconciliation with God and man.

As believers, we also can (and certainly do) have guilty feelings when we sin. True feelings of guilt come as we understand that what we have done would bring God's righteous judgment were it not for the cross and the Advocate we have in Christ Jesus. Because all your sin was paid for at the cross, there is grace super-abounding when you sin. When God looks at you, He sees Christ and His sacrifice for your sin.

But where sin abounded, grace abounded much more.

Romans 5:20 (NKJV)

Guilty feelings come as you realize you have sinned and violated God's principles. This might be more accurately described as conviction.

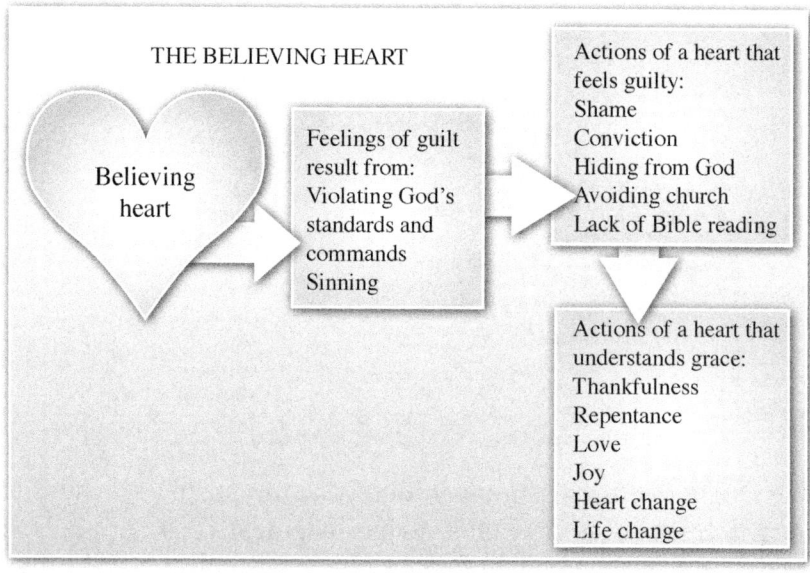

Oswald Chambers: "Conviction of sin is one of the rarest things that ever strikes a man. It is the threshold of an understanding of God. Jesus Christ said that when the Holy Spirit came He would convict of sin, and when the Holy Spirit rouses the conscience and brings him into the presence of God, it is not his relationship with men that bothers him, but his relationship with God."

Conviction of sin is not vague, it is specific. It is aimed at exposing the sinfulness of the heart and the actions and words that flow from it. The Holy Spirit convicts the Christian of sin, and urges repentance.

When you respond by admitting and confessing your sin, and then turn toward living God's way, you are built up spiritually. This is evidence of your salvation and growing faith.

On the other hand, you can have guilty feelings and yet not be guilty of a sin. This is often called "false guilt". False guilt results from fearing the cruel, heartless, and unrighteous judgment of man or becoming aware that you have violated human standards. They are not standards that are found in Scripture, but are extra-biblical rules imposed on you by others. In other words, you may not have violated any biblical principle, but someone has judged your be-havior as wrong. You feel guilt, as though you had sinned by doing something you have been told is wrong.

These standards are based on opinion and/or preference rather than Scripture, and they are changeable so you never know when you are offending someone!

Living under false guilt is a major contributor to depression. False guilt brings a desire to be further away from God because of a sense of shame. False guilt will result in fear of condemnation and judgment and bring a desire to please people at all costs. People who live to please others become idolaters, wanting to please man rather than God.

False guilt affects the relationships we have with others, too. It ruins the fellowship God intends for us to have with each other.

♥*Heart Work*

As you work through guilty feelings, you can ask these questions of yourself and those involved in the situation:

Can the person who has accused me of wrongdoing show me in the Bible how I sinned?

Have I sinned in my thought life?

Have I sinned against someone in action by retaliating?

Have I sinned against someone in speech by cursing, degrading, or insulting them?

If your answers are "no", then it is evidence that you can feel guilty and not be guilty of anything.

To illustrate the point, consider what is known as survivor's guilt. It is typically experienced by people who lived through a tragedy while others perished.

Soldiers who return home from war where their buddies perished in battle suffer with this, as well as those who lived through the 9/11 tower collapse or the Asian tsunamis. They are not guilty of anything, but they feel guilty for surviving when so many others died.

Another type of false guilt is one in which another person tries to cause you to accept responsibility for someone else's sin. This is known as blame shifting. Some examples would be: "I am mad and it is your fault": "You made me hit you": "If you wouldn't have done this, I wouldn't have done that." Blame shifting is when a battered wife is told she "got what she deserved" after her husband abandons restraint and beats her bloody. It's when a rape victim is told "she was asking for it." No woman asks to be raped. A child may be told by her violator that it is her fault that the adult desires her sexually. Blame shifting can occur in a case of incest when the other parent accuses the child of being the instigator in the incestuous relationship and sides with the abuser.

None of these guilt-inducing situations are based on truth. The offenders are attempting to soothe their own guilt by shifting the blame for their behavior onto the victim. The victim who believes the offender and takes the blame experiences a sense of false guilt. Many people spend years trying to figure out what they did that caused someone to treat them that way. Although people make foolish choices in friendships, participate in dangerous activities, or are immodest in their dress, the victim cannot make the perpetrator do anything. We are each responsible for our own actions.

Are you burdened under a false sense of guilt? Some clues that you may be struggling with false guilt include:

> * A desire to remain in seclusion, staying away from family and friends.
> * Attempting to hide from God by avoiding church, fellowship, Bible reading.
> * Seeking solace in drugs or alcohol.

If you find yourself hiding in any of these ways, I urge you to repent and put these things away from you. If you are a believer, take steps to reconnect with your Christian family.

Curing the Guilty Heart

If you are not a believer in Jesus Christ, this is the only place to begin. Becoming spiritually connected with God through the Lord Jesus Christ removes the stain of sin and its guilt and immediately places you in right fellowship with God the Father. Once this relationship has been established, guilt is no longer necessary.

Where is another God like you, who pardons the sins of the survivors among his people? You cannot stay angry with your people forever, because you delight in showing mercy. Once again you will have compassion on us. You will trample our sins under your feet and throw them into the depths of the ocean!
Micah 7:18-19 (NLT)

"I, even I, am he who blots out your transgressions, for my own sake, and remembers your sins no more."
Isaiah 43:25 (NIV)

Where There is No Sin, There is No Guilt Before God!

Some use the Scriptures to beat themselves up or to condemn themselves. The entire New Testament is a picture of God's grace to the believer and is to be read with grace in mind at all times.

You are free forever from condemnation by God or anyone else (Romans 8:1). You have been chosen in Christ before the foundation of the world to be holy and blameless in His sight (Ephesians 1:4); you have been redeemed, forgiven, and are a recipient of his lavish grace (Ephesians 1:7, 8). This should cause you to jump up and shout, "Praise the Lord!"

When you see yourself as God sees you, in light of how God Himself describes you in His own Word, your perspective changes dramatically and there is hope!

♥ *Heart Work*
Write out the things that are true about you from Romans 8:1; Ephesians 1:4, 7-8.

If you are greatly burdened by guilt, for immediate comfort, meditate on the following truths:

Nothing can ever separate me from His love.

And we know that God causes everything to work together for the good of those who love God and are called according to his purpose for them. For God knew his people in advance, and he chose them to become like his Son, so that his Son would be the firstborn, with many brothers and sisters. And having chosen them, he called them to come to him. And he gave them right standing with himself, and he promised them his glory.

What can we say about such wonderful things as these? If God is for us, who can ever be against us? Since God did not spare even his own Son but gave him up for us all, won't God, who gave us Christ, also give us everything else? Who dares accuse us whom God has chosen for his own? Will God? No! He is the one who has given us right standing with himself. Who then will condemn us? Will Christ Jesus? No, for he is the one who died for us and was raised to life for us and is sitting at the place of highest honor next to God, pleading for us.

Can anything ever separate us from Christ's love? Does it mean he no longer loves us if we have trouble or calamity, or are persecuted, or are hungry or cold or in danger or threatened with death? (Even the Scriptures say, "For your sake we are killed every day; we are being slaughtered like sheep.") No, despite all these things, overwhelming victory is ours through Christ, who loved us.

And I am convinced that nothing can ever separate us from his love. Death can't, and life can't. The angels can't, and the demons can't. Our fears for today, our worries about tomorrow, and even the powers of hell can't keep God's love away. Whether we are high above the sky or in the deepest ocean, nothing in all creation will ever be able to separate us from the love of God that is revealed in Christ Jesus our Lord.

Romans 8:28-39 (NLT)

♥ *Heart Work*
Write out the things that are true about you from Romans 8:28-39.

He will never leave you or abandon you (Hebrews 13:5).

♥ *Heart Work*
Write out the things that are true about you from Hebrews 13:5.

I bear no guilt or condemnation before God.

So now there is no condemnation for those who belong to Christ Jesus.

Romans 8:1 (NLT)

♥ *Heart Work*
Write out the things that are true about you from Romans 8:1.

125

The burden of unconfessed sin which brings feelings of guilt will feed feelings of depression. These feelings are intended to spur you on toward reconciliation with others. If you know that you have sinned against another person, make a plan to reconcile with them as soon as possible. Some people find it helpful to make a list of people they might have sinned against and then contact them to confess and repent of their sin against them.

Unfortunately, many times these issues have been glossed over or left to fester for a long time so that bitterness and resentment has built up. Do not let this discourage you from pressing forward! To clear your conscience, you must confess your sin to the ones you have sinned against and ask for their forgiveness.

Steps to asking for Forgiveness

• Go in person if at all possible. (If the sin involves an issue of immorality and the other party is married, please see the section below prior to taking this step!)

• Confess your sin in specific words to the one you have offended. You might say something like this: "(Name), I am sorry for sinning against you by (name the specific action or words you spoke). I know it has been a long time (if it has been), but I want you to know that I am sorry for (name the action or words), and would like to ask you to please forgive me."

• If they grant you forgiveness, thank them and go your way. If they want an explanation, be careful not to justify your previous actions or words, but stick to the main point of how you were wrong.

There is always great emotional danger in confessing our sin to another person because there is no guarantee that the person will forgive us. They may become hostile or hurtful to us. If this is the response, you must receive it, accept it, and thank the person for his or her time. You are not responsible for the response, only for doing your part to confess and ask for forgiveness. These steps will clear your conscience and relieve the guilt you feel.

If your sin against a person was in your thought life, you do not need to confess that to the person you thought badly about. The rule of thumb I learned from a former pastor is that the scope of confession is only as great as the scope of offense. Others can't read your mind or see in your heart; only God can. If your sin involved impure thoughts, cursing another in your mind, coveting what belongs to someone else, or another sinful thought, then these should be confessed to God alone.

If your sin involved immorality, such as adultery or an extra-marital emotional involvement, DO NOT call this person's home, cell phone, or contact them by electronic means or through the mail. You do not want to complicate matters for the other person. This situation requires much wisdom, and I would suggest that you get the help of your pastor or a biblical counselor before proceeding.

Before you venture forth, ask God's help and blessing on this decision you have made. You may want to begin with a prayer similar to this one:

Dear Father God, I can see that I am carrying around a load of guilt that I need to relieve myself of. I confess to You, Lord, the areas of my life where I have sinned against other people (list them to the best of your ability). Help me to be courageous enough to go to these people and confess my sin to them and ask their forgiveness, and help them, Lord, to forgive me. Help me to be wise in this process so I don't cause anyone undue pain or heartache.

Lord, I also see that I am carrying around guilt for things I have not done, that were not sins I committed. Help me, Lord, to recognize when guilt is being imposed on me that is not mine to own. Help me to learn to see that those who do this are hurting too, and help me to be wise and brave enough to lovingly correct them so they might learn and grow too. Thank You, Lord that the guilt, shame, and stain for all my sin was taken care of at Calvary. Thank You for Jesus, who has made me white as snow and who always stands as my Advocate before You. In His name I pray, Amen.

Chapter 10
The Faithless Heart

A popular Christian singer/songwriter has this lyric in one of her songs:

> "Faithless heart, be far away from me,
>   Playing games inside my head
>   That nobody else can see..." [1]

Because I find this area of Christian living to be so critical, especially as it relates to depression, I intend to "park" here for a while.

What does it mean to be faithless as a Christian? I looked up the word at dictionary.com and found these results:

1. Not true to duty or obligation; disloyal
2. Having no religious faith
3. Unworthy of faith or trust; unreliable

Synonyms: faithless, unfaithful, false, disloyal, traitorous, treacherous, perfidious. These adjectives mean not true to duty or obligation. Faithless and unfaithful imply failure to adhere to promises, obligations, or allegiances. False emphasizes deceitfulness. One who is disloyal betrays an allegiance. Treacherous suggests a propensity for betraying trust or faith. Perfidious suggests vileness of behavior and often deceitfulness.

No real Christians would describe themselves in the ways above, but we all seem to struggle with having faith at times. We may struggle when someone we love becomes ill with terminal cancer or when we are short on money and a big bill is due to be paid. We may even struggle when we do something we think is God's will and the whole thing turns out disastrous. In these times we wonder, where is God?

---

[1] Faithless Heart lyrics © Sony/ATV Music Publishing LLC, Warner/Chappell Music, Inc.

Your Christian friends (or maybe you) have more severe pain, more severe trials, and more rotten things happening than ever before! It can be physical pain (disease and injury), or it can be life pain (lost jobs, car accidents, slander, failed relationships), with friends and relatives suffering great and deep hurts. So much of it seems unexplainable and illogical, and you ask, "Why isn't God doing something to fix this mess?"

Life wears on you and you feel beaten down and weary. You have been so often frightened by circumstances in your life that you are fearful of what comes next because something always comes next.

You wait for the supernatural to occur, some suspension of natural law that will fix the problem. It could be a bag of money on your front porch or a miracle cure for the one you love. And when it doesn't happen, you loudly proclaim, "God is not fair!"

If you are honest with yourself, you really don't like the alternative to the supernatural magical fix because it takes wisdom, work, and time. Like most people, you want the quick fix that is done to you or for you. You want a spectacular save, where God swoops in at the last moment and rescues you. When it doesn't happen, you become angry and decide that God is not trustworthy.

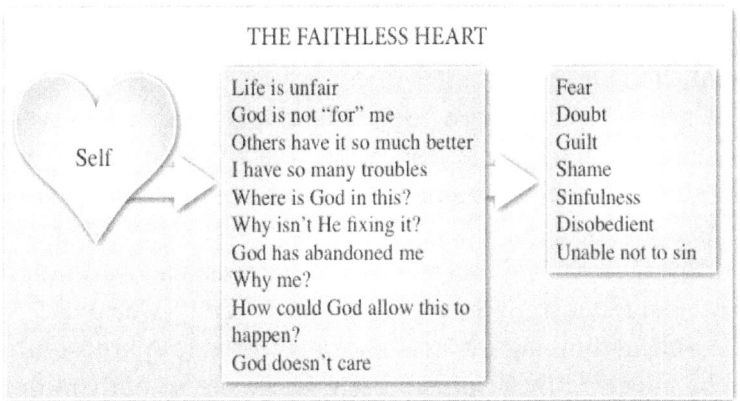

THE FAITHLESS HEART

| Self | Life is unfair
God is not "for" me
Others have it so much better
I have so many troubles
Where is God in this?
Why isn't He fixing it?
God has abandoned me
Why me?
How could God allow this to happen?
God doesn't care | Fear
Doubt
Guilt
Shame
Sinfulness
Disobedient
Unable not to sin |

The truth is that God is not obligated to "perform" the way you want Him to. He is the Master; you and I are the servants.

♥ Heart Work
How many of the heart attitudes described above are similar to those you routinely have?

If the heart attitudes above appear to describe your thoughts, beliefs, and desires I might not conclude that you lack faith in God's saving grace, but that you lack faith in God's faithfulness to you! You most likely do not apply the full definition of faithlessness to yourself, but you do apply it to God! In your faithless heart, you have concluded that He is the one who is not true to His duty or obligations; that He is disloyal to you; that He is unworthy of your faith or trust; that He is unreliable. My brothers and sisters, this should not be.

Thinking biblically leads us to conclude that God is sovereign (possessing supreme power), omniscient (all-knowing), omnipresent (everywhere all at once), and omnipotent (all-powerful). God is always aware, always in control, always navigating events and circumstances of life.

Human emotions tell us that God is a casual observer of life; that He does not or must not care about suffering. Biblical thinking reminds us that in each event He is working out good for the be-liever who loves him. Each event is completely purposeful, as well as intricately planned and guided by Him.

Emotions tell us that it is wrong to let people suffer in this way. After listening to a conversation similar to this one, a friend once said, "God is mean."

Can you really trust God when misfortune or adversity strikes? Can you really trust God when your life is filled with pain? Emotions answer with a resigned, "What choice do I have?" Do you find yourself in the default position of, "If I don't believe that God is trustworthy, then what?" Emotions want an immediate bail-out from adversity and relief from the pain. You just want it to be over.

Biblical thinking reminds us that suffering is purposeful and should be expected by believers because we are sojourners in this wicked world. Biblical thinking also tells us that it is contrary to the character of God to passively and casually observe human suffering. God is active and involved in our suffering.

Many times I hear counselees say that if they only understood what God was doing, they would feel better. We long for understanding when we are suffering. We believe that if God would pull back the curtain and let us peek into the future and see how this all turns out, we could cope with it better.

The faithless heart is a heart that lacks trust in God and His sovereignty. This is essentially a character assassination of God!

♥ Heart Work

Look again at the synonyms for unfaithful. When you react and respond emotionally, can you see how you are actually saying that God is not following through on His promises to you? Do you understand that you are actually saying that God is betraying our trust in Him?

Do you realize that you are saying that God is deceitful and treacherous? If you do not believe that God is faithful and trustworthy, then where is your hope?

Can you see how your thinking has a tremendous effect on your life? Write your response to this revelation in your notebook.

There is a close relationship between what you think and believe, and how you feel! If you have no faith or trust that God is who He says He is in the Bible, then you will struggle mightily with depression. You will be tossed about by the trials of life, and see yourself as a victim of everything. You will be, as James says, unstable in all you do (James 1:6).

So, you see, it is impossible to please God without faith. Anyone who wants to come to him must believe that there is a God and that he rewards those who sincerely seek him.

Hebrews 11:6 (NLT)

Curing the Faithless Heart

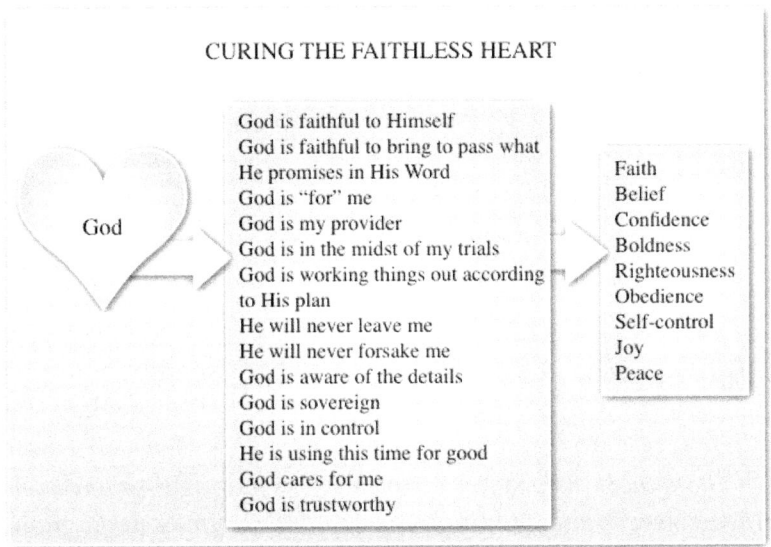

CURING THE FAITHLESS HEART

God

God is faithful to Himself
God is faithful to bring to pass what
He promises in His Word
God is "for" me
God is my provider
God is in the midst of my trials
God is working things out according
to His plan
He will never leave me
He will never forsake me
God is aware of the details
God is sovereign
God is in control
He is using this time for good
God cares for me
God is trustworthy

Faith
Belief
Confidence
Boldness
Righteousness
Obedience
Self-control
Joy
Peace

The truth is, God can be trusted in times of adversity. God is trustworthy— not for what He does but for who He is! Trustworthiness is a part of the very fabric of who God is.

God, who has called you into fellowship with his Son Jesus Christ our Lord, is faithful.

1 Corinthians 1:9 (NIV)

God, who calls you, is faithful...

1 Thessalonians 5:24 (NLT)

The unfailing love of the LORD never ends! By his mercies we have been kept from complete destruction. Great is his faithfulness; his mercies begin afresh each day.

Lamentations 3:22-23 (NLT)

Your unfailing love will last forever. Your faithfulness is as enduring as the heavens.

Psalm 89:2 (NLT)

O LORD God Almighty! Where is there anyone as mighty as you, LORD? Faithfulness is your very character.

Psalm 89:8 (NLT)

But I will not take my love from him, nor will I ever betray my faithfulness.

Psalm 89:33 (NIV)

If we are faithless, he will remain faithful, for he cannot disown himself.

2 Timothy 2:13 (NIV)

My faithfulness and unfailing love will be with him...

Psalm 89:24 (NLT)

So then, those who suffer according to God's will should commit themselves to their faithful Creator and continue to do good.

1 Peter 4:19 (NIV)

When the cupboard is empty and the bank account is too, you may have a hard time imagining how you will see God's faithfulness and how He will provide for your needs. You may get angry when God doesn't do things the way you think He ought to, but that is because you want to control your circumstances. You want to be your own sovereign. You become angry and depressed because in your view, God is not caring for or about you.

The truth is, God always cares for you. Sometimes His caring for you means hard work instead of a hand-out. Sometimes His caring for you means you will suffer for a while as God patiently teaches you a life lesson.

God does move his creation in ways we do not see to act on our behalf. Perhaps you can recall when a financial need was only brought to the Lord, and God met the need through people who were prompted to give or serve without knowing the situation. The sick are healed, marriages are restored, and the lost are redeemed in ways beyond our ability to intervene or understand. We serve a faithful God!

But now, O Israel, the LORD who created you says: "Do not be afraid, for I have ransomed you. I have called you by name; you are mine. When you go through deep waters and great trouble, I will be with you. When you go through rivers of difficulty, you will not drown! When you walk through the fire of oppression, you will not be burned up; the flames will not consume you. For I am the LORD, your God, the Holy One of Israel, your Savior.

Isaiah 43:1-3 (NLT)

From the fullness of his grace we have all received one blessing after another.

John 1:16 (NIV)

You may not believe you could withstand the hardship of having a disease, or a loved one dying, but I say to you that God's grace will overflow in time of need. God doesn't allow us to "bank" grace for a time of need. You can't get it in advance and store it up for the day you need it. God promises to be present with His grace overflowing when we are in need. Upon reflection, I would describe the experience of grace as a supernatural ability to bear up under something that would otherwise crush or kill us. It presents itself as strength and an undergirding of power that cannot be seen by the one in the midst of the fire, but is seen by those observing the recipient of that extraordinary grace.

Grace comes through faith in God—faith in His power, His person, and His promises.

So then faith comes by hearing, and hearing by the word of God.

Romans 10:17 (NKJV)

God has graciously given us the answer in His Word to our most overriding question when we suffer—the question of "why". We find it in the first chapter of the book of James. I have provided the text for you and combined several versions to emphasize my points.

Dear brothers and sisters, whenever trouble comes your way, let it be an opportunity for joy. For when your faith is tested, your endurance has a chance to grow. So let it grow, for when your endurance is fully developed, you will be strong in character and ready for anything.

If you need wisdom—if you want to know what God wants you to do— ask him, and he will gladly tell you. He will give you wisdom liberally and He does not resent your asking. But when you ask him, be sure that you ask in faith and really expect him to answer, for a mind that doubts God's faithfulness to act and answer is as unsettled as a wave of the sea that is driven and tossed by the wind. People like that should not expect to receive anything in the way of an answer from the Lord. They can't make up their minds if they believe God or not. They waver back and forth in everything they do and are generally unstable.

James 1:1-8

Trials increase our stamina, our endurance, our perseverance, and our tenacity. They drive us to our knees in prayer.

We suffer for the purpose of sanctification; for the purpose of revealing Christ in us, the hope of glory. When we suffer and undergo trials, it can make us more like Christ. Trials give us backbone and strength and, above all, they increase our faith in God and His faithfulness.

My dear ones, do not fight against God in these trials. God is hard at work in your life through them. Believe Him and trust Him. Several times in this book I have asked you to pray a prayer of commitment or change. I ask you to do the same right now regarding your lack of faith in God. As before, you may use the prayer below as a pattern to follow.

Dear gracious Heavenly Father, what You say is true. Your people do undergo more severe and more frequent, more unexplainable, and more deeply felt pain and troubles in this life than we expect we will. You tell me to call upon You in the day of trouble and You will deliver me that I might honor You (Psalm 50:15). Help me, O God, to view these adverse circumstances of my life through the eyes of faith, not the eyes of logic. Help me to find the faith to trust You in Your Word. I admit and recognize that Your plan—and Your ways of working out Your plan—are usually beyond my ability to understand. Help me to trust You when I don't understand. Help me to trust You when the day is dark and the situation looks hopeless. Help me to remember that Your providence, Your glory, and Your good are never at odds with one another, and You never sacrifice one of these for the other. Help me to remember to be thankful in my trials. Thank You that You are continuously at work in every aspect and every moment of my life and that You are bringing about good in me. I pray these things for Your glory alone! In Jesus' Name, Amen.

You must now begin to act in faith, believing that God will answer your prayer. For the depressed person, this means that the pity party is over. You have to climb out of that hole you have been sitting in and begin to live life by faith. Recognize that no plan of God's can be stopped, frustrated, or upset.

♥ *Heart Work*

Do a Bible study on the attributes of God, with an emphasis on His faithfulness. Find 52 verses about the faithfulness of God, and memorize one per week.

When the faithless thoughts begin in your mind, put them off and recite the Scripture that you have committed to memory. Then, put on an attitude of faith, testifying to what God has done and is doing in your life and in the lives of others.

As you begin to see evidence of God's faithfulness in your life, write about it in your notebook.

But it is good for me to draw near to God; I have put my trust in the Lord God, that I may declare all Your works.

Psalm 73:28 (NKJV)

137

Chapter 11
The Fearful Heart

Many people have fears. I would dare say all of us have a fear of one thing or another. I have learned that there are reasonable and legitimate reasons for fear. However, some of our fears are not so reasonable. For some, fear makes their world a smaller and smaller place until they are house-bound. They become paralyzed by the unknown. Eventually, they are too fearful to leave their perceived safe and protected environment.

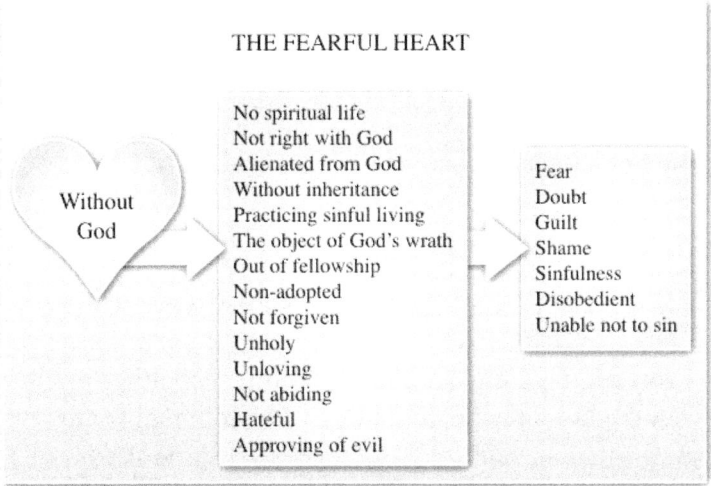

THE FEARFUL HEART

Without God

No spiritual life
Not right with God
Alienated from God
Without inheritance
Practicing sinful living
The object of God's wrath
Out of fellowship
Non-adopted
Not forgiven
Unholy
Unloving
Not abiding
Hateful
Approving of evil

Fear
Doubt
Guilt
Shame
Sinfulness
Disobedient
Unable not to sin

People who struggle with feelings of depression often say they are fearful. They may be afraid of not getting better, or of being too far gone to snap out of it. They may fear that something in the past will come back to haunt him, or that some disaster will overtake them in the future.

♥ *Heart Work*
Are you fearful?

What are you afraid of? Write about it in your notebook.

If you struggle with fear, take comfort in the knowledge that fear can be addressed biblically, and when it is, you can experience freedom from living in its grip.

Here are three common fear-based thought groups that can lead to depression:

•	What-if thoughts about the future
•	If-only thoughts and regrets about the past
•	I should/should not have: Regrets about my actions, words, or decisions

The first group we will look at is the common group of what-if thoughts. What-if thoughts steal your peace, joy, and contentment in the present because they attempt to project or see into the future. What-ifs can be either positive (what if I get that new job?) or negative (what if I have cancer?). Depending on the projections, your thoughts take you down a path that leads to rejoicing and happiness, or sorrow and depression.

♥ Heart Work

Write your "what-if" thoughts and fears in your notebook. How realistic are they?

Do you think these thoughts feed or cause your depression?

What have you done to try to overcome your "what-if" fears?

You can take any situation and forecast either joyful or depressive thoughts. The danger is that what-if thoughts are not based on what is true and real; therefore, they are in violation of Philippians 4:8:

Fix your thoughts on what is true and honorable and right. Think about things that are pure and lovely and admirable. Think about things that are excellent and worthy of praise. Keep putting into practice all you learned from me and heard from me and saw me doing, and the God of peace will be with you.

Philippians 4:8-9 (NLT)

When your thoughts are based on what-if, you will find no peace. You will find anxieties about the future (what if the worst happens?) and discontentment in the present (what if I had this or that? Wouldn't I be better off?).

The Lord tells us to keep our thoughts grounded in today.

So don't worry about tomorrow, for tomorrow will bring its own worries. Today's trouble is enough for today.
Matthew 6:34 (NLT)

Your heavenly Father already knows all your needs, and he will give you all you need from day to day if you live for him and make the Kingdom of God your primary concern.
Matthew 6:32b-33 (NLT)

What-if fears are time stealers and joy stealers. What responsibilities are you avoiding or not completing because of fear of what might or could happen? What complications does this bring into your life? (How has this changed your life?)

Another thief is to have if-only thoughts about the past. If-only thoughts are based on regret, guilt, shame, sorrow and even self-pity. We all have regrets about the past. You may believe that your past actions have altered the course of your life forever. You may believe that because of what you have done, God could never use you and no one else would want you.

The apostle Paul had much to say about the temptation to live in the past.

...I used to scoff at the name of Christ. I hunted down his people, harming them in every way I could. But God had mercy on me because I did it in ignorance and unbelief. Oh, how kind and gracious the Lord was! He filled me completely with faith and the

love of Christ Jesus. This is a true saying, and everyone should believe it: Christ Jesus came into the world to save sinners— and I was the worst of them all. But that is why God had mercy on me, so that Christ Jesus could use me as a prime example of his great patience with even the worst sinners. Then others will realize that they, too, can believe in him and receive eternal life.

1 Timothy 1:12-16 (NLT)

Perhaps you are one with a past that is not honorable. In this sin-sick society in which we live, it has become much more difficult to avoid seduction by the pleasures of the world. Many have fallen prey to various life-dominating sins (drugs, immorality, etc.) before trusting Christ, and even after, but have come to repentance and changed their way of life. The memories are sometimes hard to live with, and the pain of the life you once lived may be vivid. I imagine it was this way for Paul at times too. He had much to say about what to do with the thoughts of the past and left us an example of how to handle them:

No, dear brothers and sisters, I am still not all I should be, but I am focusing all my energies on this one thing: Forgetting the past and looking forward to what lies ahead, I strain to reach the end of the race and receive the prize for which God, through Christ Jesus, is calling us up to heaven.

Philippians 3:13-15 (NLT)

What a testimony!

♥ *Heart Work*

Does it surprise you to learn about Paul's sordid past?

Does Paul model an "if only" way of thinking?

After looking at his example, do you think that you have to be a prisoner of your past?

Re-read 1 Timothy 1:12-16 and Philippians 3:13-15. What is the key to Paul's ability to move past his past?

What wisdom is there for you in the words of Paul? Write your personal application in your notebook.

Other if-only thoughts are rooted in wishful thinking: a desire to alter the present through magical means. "If only I could win the lottery." These thoughts reveal great dissatisfaction with the present and often reveal discontentment with God's sovereignty and provision.

♥ *Heart Work*
What are your "if-only" desires?

Take a few minutes and think about whether these thoughts contribute to your feelings of depression. Write out how your thoughts are creating discontentment and dissatisfaction.

The final area of fearful thoughts is, "I should have/shouldn't have." These thoughts are usually related to life-decisions a person has made that they now regret due to the consequences they will experience. They are closely related to "if only" thoughts and focus backward on events and things that cannot be changed.

To forget what is behind you, as Paul did (Philippians 3:13-15) is to truly put it on the cross and remember it no more. It is coming to a full acceptance that you have been completely cleansed by the blood of Christ and are completely justified in the sight of God. It is to reckon yourself dead to that way of life and alive to the new life you have in Christ (Romans 6:11).

But you may have discovered that your mind is not so quick to forget your past, and neither are people. It can take more time than you would like for people in your life to stop thinking of the old you, and to see the person you are in Christ. Satan also has his hand in that game, as he is quick to remind you of your past.

One major area of regret is over sexual impurity. Immorality is rampant in the world and many who have repented after partaking in the pleasures of the world (pre-marital sex, adultery, pornography, and other lusts of the flesh), continue to live with the negative emotional consequences of those actions. Sexual thoughts can be diffcult to remove from your mind. They seem to have blazed a deep trail on your brain and you feel shame and guilt about your past. Fear is closely connected to the guilt and shame of exposure.

Paul may have struggled with the thoughts of his past, and he penned a terrific passage for us to memorize:

For though we live in the world, we do not wage war as the world does. The weapons we fight with are not the weapons of the world. On the contrary, they have divine power to demolish strongholds. We demolish arguments and every pretension that sets itself up against the knowledge of God, and we take captive every thought to make it obedient to Christ.

2 Corinthians 10:3-5 (NIV)

Taking every thought captive means that you don't allow your thoughts to dwell there anymore. When your mind wanders in the direction of the past, remind yourself of biblical truth. You are most likely not the same person you were when those things were appealing to you. God has been at work in your heart, renewing your mind so that you are no longer willing to participate in those deeds of the flesh. In fact, your disdain and other negative reactions to such things are evidence of the changes within proof of the changes within you!

♥ *Heart Work*
Take a moment and think about how your thoughts have changed with respect to some of the worldly things you used to enjoy. Write them in your notebook, on a Then/Now chart like this:

Then	**Now**
(sinful things I used to love)	(What I think and believe about those things today)

Philippians 4:8 also tells us to meditate on what is pure, lovely, admirable, excellent or praiseworthy. The exploits of the past that were ungodly are none of those things.

You must renew your mind with the Word of God. Memorize Scripture so that you can recall it when sinful or fearful thoughts arise. You cannot fight these thoughts in your own power, nor do you need to. God has provided your weaponry!

Fear of Man

Another major area of fear in a depressed person is what is known as fear of man. I have referred to this elsewhere in the chapter on Idolatry but I want to go a little deeper here because it is so relevant and important for a person who struggles with fear and depression.

It is important to note that depression is not always visible on the outside. A person can be thinking very depressing thoughts related to how they feel about themselves, yet keep them hidden. While they may deny it when asked, their sense of self-worth is very important to them. They are fearful of not being well thought of, and ultimately they live for the approval of people. This is known as having fear of man.

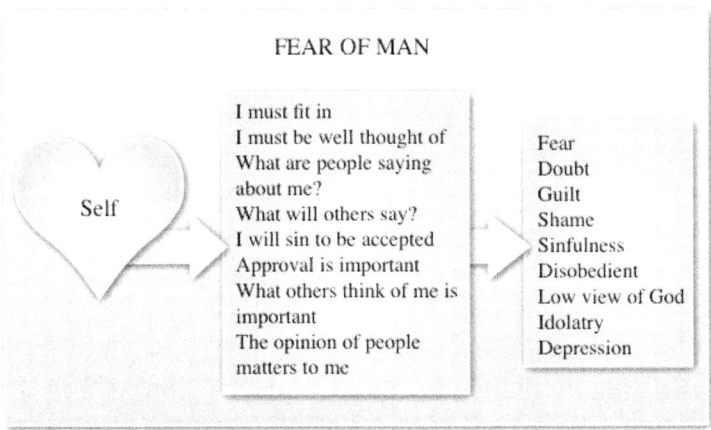

FEAR OF MAN

Self

I must fit in
I must be well thought of
What are people saying about me?
What will others say?
I will sin to be accepted
Approval is important
What others think of me is important
The opinion of people matters to me

Fear
Doubt
Guilt
Shame
Sinfulness
Disobedient
Low view of God
Idolatry
Depression

Fear of man is not always easy to detect, because those who struggle with it often have the best attitudes about everything! They can be the go-to people who are everywhere doing everything in your churches. Their lives can be full of activity, and so they are not looked upon as being depressed. They are considered to be self-sacrificing and service-oriented because they rarely say no to anything. They typically put forth their best efforts and seem determined not to let anyone down.

Some people who struggle with fear of man issues appear to be happy and content, especially while they are serving others. This is one reason family and friends are so surprised to learn of depression in such a person.

The reality is, many people pleasers are internally tormented, and are prisoners of the good opinions of those people they serve. Ed Welch, in his fantastic book, <u>When People Are Big and God is Small</u>, says this about fear of man: "It includes being afraid of some-one, but it extends to holding someone in awe, being controlled or mastered by people, worshiping other people, putting your trust in people, or needing people. People become 'our idol of choice.'"

♥ Heart Work
Does this describe you?

Those with fear of man issues describe themselves as being shy, having love or approval needs, people-pleasers, having an empty love tank/cup, or may have picked up the term co-dependent somewhere along the way. They truly do not understand that this way of living is grossly sinful before God.

When people are big, their opinions are so very important to us. We have to "fit in," and we believe that we have to belong. I struggled with this whole area so much as I was growing up! I desperately wanted to fit in with those I perceived to be the popular kids. I literally agonized before my clothes closet each morning trying to predict what the girls would be wearing to school that day. Would it be pants or skirts? And when I would get it wrong I was crushed, and my day would be ruined. This constant approval seeking led me to do things that I had been raised to know were wrong.

Most of my adult life, I lived with a yearning to be affirmed and fit in with my unsaved family members. I wanted their approval of my lifestyle and beliefs, which I never received. I was always seeking the positive strokes that the approval of others would bring me. The fear of rejection was so great, I adapted to whomever and whatever would bring me the praise of my peers. Peer pressure is another term for fear of man.

♥ Heart Work
Are you a people pleaser? Write out the fears you have about not measuring up to the expectations of other people.

Have you compromised your beliefs to fit in with others? In what ways?

Do you recognize this as idolatry?

If you recognize yourself as this kind of idolater, rejoice! There is hope for you in Christ to change from one who has an overly high view of man to someone who has a high view of God. Having a proper view of God comes from seeing Him the way the Bible describes Him to be. Even a quick study of the names of God reveals His nature and His character, and all speak of His goodness, righteousness, justice, holiness, power, and love.

There is no one holy like the LORD, indeed, there is no one besides You...

1 Samuel 2:2 (NIV)

...give thanks to Your holy name

1 Chronicles 16:35 (NIV)

...I will ascribe righteousness to my Maker.

Job 36:3 (NIV)

When we elevate the opinions of people over the Person of God we are headed for disastrous waters. Our focus is to be on the worship of God, and on living to reveal Him to others that they might also be drawn to Him through our lives and witness.

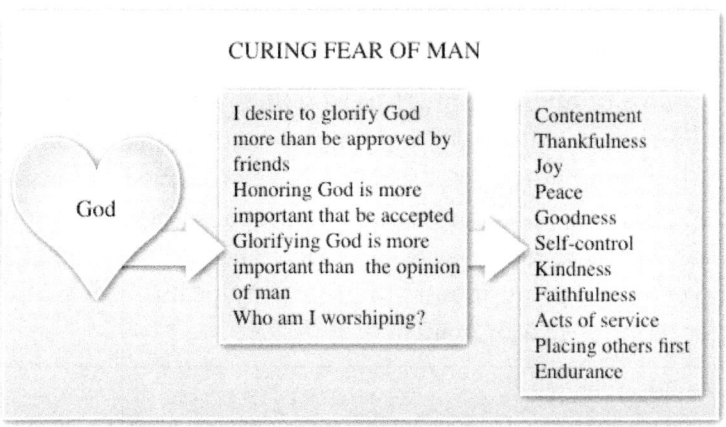

CURING FEAR OF MAN

God

I desire to glorify God more than be approved by friends
Honoring God is more important that be accepted
Glorifying God is more important than the opinion of man
Who am I worshiping?

Contentment
Thankfulness
Joy
Peace
Goodness
Self-control
Kindness
Faithfulness
Acts of service
Placing others first
Endurance

As you can see, addressing fear of man issues takes the same course as addressing the heart of idolatry because these are one and the same issue.

Having a fear of God, meaning reverence and awe of Him, becomes our life's passion. Developing a reverence for God over fear of man requires a commitment to God that goes beyond the superficial. It becomes more important to do what is honorable in God's eyes regardless of how others think of us or our decisions and opinions. In our day and age, this may mean taking a stand against a politically correct position or admitting you actually read and believe the teachings of the Bible. Having a high view of God puts what the Bible says above the opinion of man.

Curing the Heart of Fear

You will keep in perfect peace him whose mind is steadfast, because he trusts in you.

Isaiah 26:3 (NIV)

Meditate on These Things:

Finally, brothers, whatever is true, whatever is noble, whatever is right, whatever is pure, whatever is lovely, whatever is admirable—if anything is excellent or praiseworthy—think about such things. Whatever you have learned or received or heard from me, or seen in me—put it into practice. And the God of peace will be with you.

Philippians 4:8-9 (NIV)

If you are practicing and meditating on what is true, lovely, pure, admirable, and so on, it is impossible to be thinking about what is false, ugly, immoral, of ill repute, and so on. When you understand that He has reconciled you to Himself (2 Corinthians 5:18-19), you realize that He reached out to you in spite of your sin and in spite of who you were, and He brought you to Himself.

Instead of praying in this section, I would like you to get out your Bible and open it to Ephesians chapter one. Take the time right now and begin to read aloud Ephesians 1:1 through 2:10. As you read, I want you to replace the pronouns (our, us, we, you, etc.) with your own name. I want you to make this personal, because it is personal. This passage of Scripture was written to you, a believer in Christ, to tell you what God has done for you and what He intends to do in you and through you. Begin reading, and may God bless your heart as you do so.

When you understand that you are God's workmanship, created in Christ Jesus to do His work which He planned beforehand for you to do, your life has a purpose.

For we are God's workmanship, created in Christ Jesus to do good works, which God prepared in advance for us to do.

Ephesians 2:10 (NIV)

♥*Heart Work*

Think about what God has for you to do in this life.

Do you recognize this as a reason to get out of bed every morning?

When you understand that you are righteous and holy before God, there no longer remains a stain from sins like abortion or adultery, and no reason to fear judgment.

You must display a new nature because you are a new person, created in God's likeness—righteous, holy, and true.

Ephesians 4:24 (NLT)

I tell you the truth, whoever hears my word and believes him who sent me has eternal life and will not be condemned; he has crossed over from death to life.

John 5:24 (NIV)

♥*Heart Work*

Do you believe that you truly are a new person in Christ?

Do you believe that the words, righteous and holy apply to you?

Do you accept that in Christ you are no longer condemned for your past, present, or your future sins?

When you understand that you are chosen and holy because of Christ, a desire arises to serve Him and to live life for His glory.

Therefore, as God's chosen people, holy and dearly loved, clothe yourselves with compassion, kindness, humility, gentleness and patience.

Colossians 3:12 (NIV)

This is frequently an area that Christians struggle to accept. The pervasiveness of performance driven/works based Christianity has led many of us to wrongly believe that God only accepts and loves us based on what we do and how well we do it.

This sets us up for living in fear—the wrong kind of fear—of God. The fear that God will "get" us if we aren't perfect in obedience and spiritual disciplines. The fear that God will judge us and not love us because we wrestle with sin. The fear that, because we still do sin, we are somehow defective and don't have enough of God or the Holy Spirit. And the most tragic of all, that God couldn't possibly love us because we are sinners.

The works we have been called to do are to be done out of love for the Lord, not fear of being struck or punished by Him. God has enabled us to accomplish the tasks and changes He set before us, and by His grace we will! You don't have to worry about being perfectly compassionate, kind, or loving. God is at work in you, and He is faithful to complete what He has begun.

When you understand that you are a child of light, you desire to begin to walk worthy of this calling you have received from God, to be a light in a dark world.

> *You are all sons of the light and sons of the day. We do not belong to the night or to the darkness.*
> 1 Thessalonians 5:5 (NIV)

When you understand that you are a partaker of Christ and that you share in His life, your life has meaning!

> *For we have become partakers of Christ if we hold the beginning of our confidence steadfast to the end...*
> Hebrews 3:14 (NKJV)

When these truths are poorly understood, you will not have these assurances or motivations to live by, and you will experience fear. Old thinking patterns may persist and lead you to continue to live life by your feelings as long as you have not replaced those patterns with truth. As a result, you will have fear.

The way to break old thinking patterns and the grip of fear is to have your mind transformed by the Word and its truths, these truths before you. That is what brings peace, hope, and joy. Consider these truths:

Jesus Christ shares with you in every detail of the suffering.

For we do not have a high priest who is unable to sympathize with our weaknesses, but we have one who has been tempted in every way, just as we are—yet was without sin.

Hebrews 4:15 (NIV)

♥ *Heart Work*

What does it mean to you that Jesus shares in every detail of your suffering?

Does knowing He has suffered and is suffering right along with you bring you comfort? Assurance?

Jesus has experienced the very temptations you experience; something that is difficult for us to grasp. Hebrews 4:15 says that He was tempted in every way! Write out your thoughts and response to this truth.

How does this help you?

God is in sovereign, loving control of every circumstance.

For you have been my hope, O Sovereign LORD, my confidence since my youth.

Psalm 71:5 (NIV)

I will come and proclaim your mighty acts, O Sovereign LORD; I will proclaim your righteousness, yours alone.

Psalm 71:16 (NIV)

But as for me, it is good to be near God. I have made the Sovereign LORD my refuge; I will tell of all your deeds.

Psalm 73:28 (NIV)

But deal well with me, O Sovereign LORD, for the sake of your own reputation! Rescue me because you are so faithful and good.

Psalm 109:21 (NLT)

O Sovereign LORD, the strong one who rescued me, you pro-tected me on the day of battle.

Psalm 140:7 (NLT)

God is our refuge and strength, an ever-present help in trouble.

Psalm 46:1 (NIV)

Let us then approach the throne of grace with confidence, so that we may receive mercy and find grace to help us in our time of need.

Hebrews 4:16 (NIV)

Do not hesitate to bring your burdens to Christ. He loves you and cares about every trial in your life. Begin today to put the things you have learned into practice. There is no time like the present, and the sooner you begin, the sooner you will be experiencing God and life in ways you never imagined!

Chapter 12
Finding Your Joy in "Christ in You."

Throughout this book you have learned about the various sin issues and attitudes of the heart typically found in those who grapple with feelings of depression. I want to leave you with a few final thoughts if you struggle with not having joy.

Your greatest joy is found in Christ alone. This is the secret to happiness in life. Jesus wanted to help the disciples understand this before he went to the cross, and like everything else in the Bible, it is meant to encourage us too.

In John 15, Jesus is speaking to His disciples. He gives them a beautiful message of comfort, love, hope, and assurance. This passage follows John 14, where he has just told them that He is going away (which they don't understand) and that He will send the Holy Spirit to guide them in truth. Jesus assures them that they will continue to grow and change in the absence of His physical presence. He uses the illustration of the vine and the branches.

"I am the true vine, and my Father is the gardener. He cuts off every branch in me that bears no fruit, while every branch that does bear fruit he prunes so that it will be even more fruitful. You are already clean because of the word I have spoken to you. Remain in me, and I will remain in you. No branch can bear fruit by itself; it must remain in the vine. Neither can you bear fruit unless you remain in me.

"I am the vine; you are the branches. If a man remains in me and I in him, he will bear much fruit; apart from me you can do nothing. If anyone does not remain in me, he is like a branch that is thrown away and withers; such branches are picked up, thrown into the fire and burned. If you remain in me and my words remain in you, ask whatever you wish, and it will be given you. This is to my Father's glory, that you bear much fruit, showing yourselves to be my disciples.

"As the Father has loved me, so have I loved you. Now remain in my love. If you obey my commands, you will remain in my love, just as I have obeyed my Father's commands and remain in his love. I have told you this so that my joy may be in you and that your joy may be complete. My command is this: Love each other as I have loved you. Greater love has no one than this, that he lay down his life for his friends."

John 15:1-13 (NIV)

The correct understanding of this passage requires a little teaching, for on the surface, it can appear confusing. Once understood, this passage brings tremendous hope! Bear with me as I explain.

Jesus is the true vine and the Father is the gardener in this passage. Two types of branches are described—branches that bear fruit and those that do not. The branches that do not bear fruit represent people who profess to believe, but their lack of fruit reveals that genuine salvation has not taken place, because there is no life in the branch. The dead branches will be gathered up by the gardener and thrown into the fire (indicating future judgment) to make way for the living branches to be clearly revealed.

The gardener prunes the living branches to enable them to bear greater fruit. The pruning process is a cutting away of things that would cause the branch to bear small, poor-quality fruit. (We could personalize the pruned branches as the sin issues that have been discussed throughout this book.) This time of discouragement and depression in your life is a pruning season. The purpose for the pruning is that God intends to produce more and better fruit in you.

We are then told, "Remain in me and I will remain in you." The word abide is used in some translations and means to remain. The remaining is evidence of genuine salvation.

The life of the branch is hidden in the attachment to the vine, and fruit is produced as a direct result. Only the branches attached to the vine will bear fruit.

Here is the application: You are the branch and you will always be attached to the vine. Your life in Christ is secure and your salvation is secure. You cannot be detached from the vine for that would mean that you could by an act of your will undo what Christ has done for you in the act of saving you. Because you are eternally attached to the vine you will produce good fruit. The Lord Jesus Christ through the Holy Spirit will reveal His life in you by the fruit you produce. The good news is that the work of fruit production is God's. It is not gained by your straining and striving.

We cannot produce genuine fruit apart from the working of the Holy Spirit. The fruit produced by human effort, while resembling the fruit of the Spirit, is counterfeit.

The fruit of the Spirit in the life of a depressed person can become:
- Peace
- Encouragement
- Endurance
- Hope
- Joy
- Perseverance through suffering sacrifice
- Service
- Loving one another
- Humility
- Meekness

You can rely on God to accomplish the good works that He began in you. This season of depression is just one part of your life in Christ and has never been out of His control. His desire for you is that you change from what you once were to the person He has prepared for you to become in Him.

He has done the hard part: He has given you peace with God, given you a new life, and placed His Spirit within you. You now have the opportunity to live out your transformation—to cooperate with what God intends to do in and through you to those around you.

As I said earlier, this place you are in is no accident; it is a divine appointment, and God intends to do something through it. This book contains practical suggestions for you to work on and apply to your life, so begin today, my friend, and I trust God will continue to give you grace and mercy on your journey!

My prayer for you:

Dear gracious heavenly Father,

My prayer for those who read this book is that you would be glorified in their lives. Please use this offering, Lord, to impact the hearts and minds of those who read it. Help them to connect how their heart affects their thoughts, beliefs, and desires, and how these things affect their lives. Father, help them to change biblically and to accomplish change that is long lasting and brings joy to their hearts and lives, and glory to Your magnificent name.

These changes are hard, dear Lord, and the path is full of the obstacles of self and pride and all that is associated with these sins. Give your children courage to stay the course. Assure them that You are indeed with them as they fight against the sinful nature and its desires. I ask You to give them the victory in Christ Jesus. Amen.

Section Two

Perspective on the Current Medical and Psychological Thinking on Depression, Chemical Imbalance, and Medication to Treat Depression

Since I wrote this book in 2006, there have been numerous advances in medical science and in the understanding of what is called "mental illness". At the time of this writing (summer of 2014) there has been an enormous shake-up in the mental health system with the release of the newest edition of the American Psychiatric Association's DSM-5 (Diagnostic and Statistical Manual of Mental Disorders, Fifth Edition). The mental health arena is a group in which the participants are consistently changing opinions based on new research (both good and bad).

When I began counseling biblically, I received calls every week from people wanting counseling for depression and other "mental illnesses". Over the years there has been a change. Few people come for help specifically for depression, but nearly all of them list depression as one of the issues they deal with. Many of them are taking psychotropic medication (drugs that act on the mind) and have been told they have a form of mental or emotional disorder. In the past, the counselee would most likely have been through some other form of counseling and their psychiatrist would have written the prescription for the medication. Today, the major-ity of my counselees tell me their prescriber was their family doctor or Physician Assistant.

Where Does Depression Come From?

The world and its "experts" tell us that depression is an ill-ness, a sickness that can be treated only by a "qualified expert". The DSM-5 classifies depression as a mental illness. Various organizations and web sites on depression state that depression is a medical illness or a disease. Consider the following quotes:

"Depression, also known as major depression, clinical depression or major depressive disorder is a medical illness that causes a constant feeling of sadness and lack of interest. Depression affects how the person feels, behaves and thinks."[1]

"Depression is an extremely complex disease."[2]

"There is no single known cause of depression. Rather, it likely results from a combination of genetic, biochemical, environmental, and psychological factors...Research indicates that depressive illnesses are disorders of the brain... important neurotransmitters—chemicals that brain cells use to communicate—appear to be out of balance."[3]

The National Institute of Mental Health says, "Some types of depression run in families, suggesting that a biological vulnerability can be inherited....In some families, major depression also seems to occur generation after generation. However, it can also occur in people who have no family history of depression. Whether inherited or not, major depressive disorder is often associated with changes in brain structures or brain function. People who have low self-esteem, who consistently view themselves and the world with pessimism or who are readily overwhelmed by stress, are prone to depression. Whether this represents a psychological predisposition or an early form of the illness is not clear." [4]

"It's not known exactly what causes depression. As with many mental illnesses, it appears a variety of factors may be involved." Eric Kandel, MD[5]

"All mental processes are brain processes, and therefore all disorders of mental functioning are biological diseases,"[6]

---

[1] http://www.medicalnewstoday.com/articles/8933.php) accessed 4/26/15

[2] http://www.webmd.com/depression/guide/causes-depression accessed 4/26/2015

[3] http://www.psychologytoday.com/basics/depression/causes accessed 4/26/15

[4] http://psychcentral.com/lib/2006/the-causes-of-depression/ (Accessed 04/26/2015)

[5] http://www.mayoclinic.com/health/depression/DS00175/DSECTION=causes (accessed 04/26/15)

[6] http://www.apa.org/monitor/2012/06/roots.aspx (Accessed 04/26/2015)

To Thomas R. Insel, MD, director of the National Institute of Mental Health, mental illnesses are no different from heart disease, diabetes or any other chronic illness. "All chronic diseases have behavioral components as well as biological components. The brain is the organ of the mind. Where else could [mental illness] be if not in the brain? The only difference here is that the organ of interest is the brain instead of the heart or pancreas. But the same basic principles apply."[7]

A Differing View

Not all quotes are stated as conclusively. Clinical psychologist Bruce Levine writes, "No biochemical, neurological, or genetic markers have been found for attention deficit disorder, depression, schizophrenia, anxiety, compulsive alcohol or drug abuse, overeating, gambling, or any other so-called mental illness, disease, or dis-order."

"At the present time, there is no diagnostic laboratory test (e.g., no blood test or brain scan) that can confirm whether you have Major Depression. However, some laboratory tests can appear abnormal during an active depressive episode…Other abnormalities in brain chemicals and hormones also occur with depression, but none of the tests examining these factors are stable, reliable, or specific enough at present to develop a foolproof way of diagnosing Major Depression."[8]

Elliot Valenstein, University of Michigan neuroscientist, writes, "Contrary to what is often claimed, no biochemical, anatomical, or functional signs have been found that reliably distinguish the brains of mental patients."[9]

"The whole disease model that underlies the DSM has been an utter scientific failure. There's not a single biological marker for any of the 300-plus disorders. What we do instead is descriptive.

---

[7]http://www.apa.org/monitor/2012/06/roots.aspx (Accessed 04/26/2015)

[8]The Course of Major Depression Rashmi Nemade, Ph.D., Natalie Staats Reiss, Ph.D., and Mark Dombeck, Ph.D. Updated: Sep 19th 2007 http://www.rvcc-inc.org/poc/view_doc.php?type=doc&id=528&cn=5

[9]http://www.ctvip.org/?p=174 (Accessed 04/26/2015)

This describing is creating a disorder and pretending it's a medical illness rather than just human behavior."[10]

Joseph Glenmullen, M.D., clinical instructor in psychiatry at Harvard Medical School, says, "A serotonin deficiency for depression has not been found. . . . Still, patients are often given the impression that a definitive serotonin deficiency in depression is firmly established."[11]

Psychotherapist Gary Greenberg, of New London, Conn., has written about the DSM for more than a decade and says the DSM disorders are "...simply collections of symptoms that some experts agree constitute mental illnesses. There's not a single diagnosis in DSM that lives up to the standards of medical diseases. If I as a therapist tell you (that) you have a mental disorder, it's not the same thing as my telling you that you have diabetes or cancer because diabetes and cancer are diseases that can be confirmed through biochemical findings. They meet the requirements for a disease in the way we generally think of a disease. There is not a single disorder in DSM-5 or any DSM that does that".[12]

Maurice Victor, M.D., Professor of Medicine and Neurology at Dartmouth Medical School; and Allan H. Ropper, M.D., Professor and Chairman of Neurology at Tufts University School of Medicine, agree: "At the present time, it must be conceded that there is no reliable biologic test for depression."[13]

God's View

The Bible records the thoughts of a depressed psalmist:

Because of your anger, my whole body is sick; my health is broken because of my sins. My guilt overwhelms me—it is a burden

---

[10]Stuart Kirk, professor emeritus of social welfare at UCLA, http://www.usatoday.com/story/news/nation/2013/05/12/dsm-psychiatry-mental-disorders/2150819/ (accessed 04/26/2015)

[11]*Prozac Backlash*, Joseph Glenmullen, (Simon & Schuster, New York, 2000), pages 197-198.

[12]http://www.usatoday.com/story/news/nation/2013/05/12/dsm-psychiatry-mental-disorders/2150819/ (Accessed 3/10/2015)

[13]http://www.antipsychiatry.org/depressi.htm, (accessed 04/26/2015)

too heavy to bear. My wounds fester and stink because of my foolish sins. I am bent over and racked with pain. My days are filled with grief. A raging fever burns within me, and my health is broken. I am exhausted and completely crushed. My groans come from an anguished heart. You know what I long for, Lord; you hear my every sigh. My heart beats wildly, my strength fails, and I am going blind. My loved ones and friends stay away, fearing my disease. Even my own family stands at a distance.

Psalm 38:3-11 (NLT)

How do we reconcile the conflicting opinions of those who say depression is an illness, others who say that claim has no basis in fact, and the words of the Bible regarding the causes and cures of depression?

In my quest to understand this complex issue, I sought out materials written by medical professionals: Medical doctors, neuroscientists, neurobiophysicists, and psychiatrists who have done extensive research on the theories about this prevalent physical and emotional state. I have quoted them extensively throughout. As you can see, some medical professionals radically disagree with the proponents of the theories of mental illnesses. Even with all the advances in medicine, neuroscience and technology, seven years after the original publication of this book, there is still no consensus on the cause of depression and other "mental illnesses", nor is there a cure. Treatment includes management of behavior and symptoms through therapy and medication, but there is no cure. There is great confusion and disagreement within the medical and scientific com-munities about depression and other mental illnesses, yet theories continue to be presented as scientific fact.

My goal is to expose you, the reader, to the alternative legitimate viewpoint on what the world calls depression and mental illness. Like my colleagues, I am greatly concerned and alarmed about the onslaught of these diagnoses. Entire segments of the population (e.g., lonely housewives, drunkards, those enslaved to sexual sin or anger, undisciplined children) are being diagnosed as mentally ill on a daily basis. An article published by The American Hospital association in January 2012 reports that half of all Americans will develop a mental disorder at some time in their lives![14] A recent ABC News blog says one in five Americans experienced some sort of mental illness in 2010.[15]

How did we get to such a place? How can it be that in the last 50 years, the world has seemingly (pardon the pun) gone mad? My assessment is that because of the influence of evolution, psychiatry, and social liberalism, our society has effectively eliminated God, standards of morality, and absolutes. Behaviors once considered deviant and immoral are being redefined as normal, or are now classified as medical conditions or illnesses by the psychological professionals. You can find them among the 5,146 conditions currently described in the Diagnostic and Statistical Manual of Mental Disorders, fifth edition (DSM-5).

Facts on the Diagnostic and Statistical Manual of Mental Disorders:

What is the DSM?

Dr. David Powlison (CCEF) calls the DSM "the definitive sourcebook for making psychiatric diagnoses."

The DSM was originally created as a way to organize psychiatric knowledge research efforts and treatment approaches. Those who revised the DSM since 1968 have claimed that each successive revision is much more scientific than its predecessor.

Why is it Controversial?

The History of the DSM and Diagnostic Reliability

The number of categories and specifiers for mood disorders has increased with each successive edition of the Diagnostic and Statistical Manual for Mental Disorders (DSM). Many of these categories and specifiers can be viewed as an effort to map the various

[14]Ronals Kessler, et al. "Lifetime Prevalence of Age-of-Onset Distributions of DSM-IV Disorders in the National Comorbidity Survey Replication, Archives of General Psychiatry Vol. 62, No. 6 (June 2005), 593-602

[15]http://abcnews.go.com/blogs/health/2012/01/19/1-in-5-americans-suffer-from-mental-illness/ (Accessed 3/10/2015)

permutations of severity and chronicity that characterize the depressive disorders.[16]

This method of "treatment" provides no clear distinction between normal and abnormal. It is also completely subjective based on how the therapist "feels" and "interprets."

It is critical that you understand the controversy that has surrounded this manual, which is now in its fifth edition. The DSM-1 was first published in 1952 by the American Psychiatric Association (APA) and contained approximately 60 disorders.[17]

The second volume, published in 1968, included 130 disorders. The DSM was originally created as a way to organize psychiatric knowledge, research efforts, and treatment approaches.[18]

The first two volumes were influenced by a therapeutic approach called psychodynamic psychotherapy, which, generally speaking, attempts to get patients to deal with painful feelings they may have buried because they think they cannot face them.[19]

In psychodynamic therapy, "the therapist normally takes an attitude of unconditional acceptance," says Heiko Ganzer, psycho-therapist and director of Phoenix Psychotherapy. "The therapist tries to develop a relationship with you, to help you discover what is going on in your unconscious mind. They do this partly by theoreti-cal knowledge [academic stuff!], partly by experience, and partly through their knowledge of themselves."[20]

---

[16]http://www.ncbi.nlm.nih.gov/pmc/articles/PMC3057920/ (accessed 3/10/15)

[17]Hana Kubota and Takeshi Matsuishi, "Major Revision of the Diagnostic and Statistical Manual of Mental Disorders (DSM)-Background of the Change and Conceptualization of Mental Disorders." http: //www.medico-pedagogy.org/dsm3summaryJ_Ewp.pdf (Accessed 04/26/2015)

[18]http://www.academyanalyticarts.org/kirk&kutchins.htm," The Academy for the Study of the Psychoanalytic Arts, http://www.academyanalyticarts.org/kirk&kutchins.htm. First printed in the Journal of Mind and Behavior, 15 (1&2), 1994, 71-86. (Accessed 04/26/2015)

[19]For a short list of therapy methods, see "What is Psychotherapy?" http://www.nimh.nih.gov/health/topics/psychotherapies/index.shtml (Accessed 04/26/2015)

[20]Heiko Ganzer, "Psychodynamic Therapy" Accessed at http://easyweb.easynet.co.uk/simplepsych/204.html (Accessed 04/26/2015)

The classification structure of early editions of the DSM was rooted in a distinction between two poles of mental disorder: psychosis and neurosis. A psychosis is a severe mental disorder characterized by a disconnect from reality. Psychoses typically involve hallucinations, delusions, and illogical thinking. A neurosis, however, is a milder mental disorder characterized by distortions of reality but not a complete break with reality. Neuroses typically involve anxiety and depression.

Author Stuart A. Kirk, professor and director of the Ph.D. program of the Department of Social Welfare, School of Public Policy and Social Research at UCLA, writes, "During the 1950s and 1960s, psychiatry and the mental health professions were confronted with many serious criticisms: the effectiveness of psychotherapy was questioned; psychiatrists were accused of over-reliance on involuntary commitment and of violating the civil liberties of citizens; and mental health professionals were criticized for failing to respond to the mental health needs of minorities and the poor and for being inattentive to the quality of institutional care.

"No challenge was as fundamental, however, as the challenges to the concept of mental illness itself. These challenges came from psychiatrists like Szasz (1960, 1961), who argued that mental illness was a myth used to disguise the bitter pill of moral conflicts. Sociologists such as Goffman (1961) and Scheff (1966) suggested that mental illness was merely another example of how society labels and controls those who do not behave; from behavioral psychologists who challenged psychiatry's fundamental reliance on intrapsychic, unobservable phenomena; and from gay activists who challenged the APA's listing of homosexuality as a mental disorder."[21]

Due to questions about the reliability of the data in the previous two editions, the DSM- III was published in 1980 and grew to a listing of 265 diagnoses. DSM-III-R (revised) was published in 1987. The DSM-III introduced diagnostic psychiatry, which was a major, lucrative shift in psychiatry. "Diagnostic psychiatry sought to categorize disorders into a defined set of disease entities with the

[21]Stuart A. Kirk and Herb Kutchins, The Myth of the Reliability of DSM http://www. academyanalyticarts.org/kirk-myth-reliability-dsm APA stands for the American Psychiatric Association.

basic premise of being a medical or biological abnormality in the brain," says Dr. Kurt Grady, speaking at the International Association of Biblical Counselors' national conference in 2005. "Similar to non-psychiatric medicine, the move to diagnostic psychiatry ensured that the financial engines of psychiatry would continue unabated. In fact, by moving into a biological hypothesis, psychiatry was able to tap into the vast, and I mean vast, financial resources of the pharmaceutical industry for furthering their biological and genetic disease-based theories and research."[22]

"Precisely because DSM-III has been described as a 'watershed document,' 'a stunning achievement,' 'a scientific revolution,' and as having brought about a 'transformation of American psychiatry, the claims of its developers deserve careful scrutiny,'" write Kirk and Kutchins.[23]

"It is often very diffcult to assess such claims because the revisions of DSM involve not one or a few central changes, but hundreds of them," they write. "No one person can possibly assess all the relevant scientific evidence for each of these changes. When there are references to evidence that is purported to justify changes, it often comes from data gathered in special field trials that are rarely available to the public until most major decisions have been made... Thus, the scientific integrity of the revision process cannot be assessed until long after a revised DSM is published. By then, the next revision is under way and criticism of the last revision appears petty or irrelevant or both. But, unless past claims by proponents of DSM are scrutinized in light of the scientific evidence that was used at the time, we are unable to evaluate the extent to which science and systematic evidence support the process of continual revision. [24]

These attacks raised serious questions about the legitimacy of psychiatry as a scientifically based profession, according to Kirk

---

[22]Kurt Grady, "Chemical Imbalances: Scientific Fact or Social Phenomenon," audio CD of lecture presented at the national conference of the International Association of Biblical Counselors (IABC) in Colorado Springs, Colorado, August 2005. For a copy of the CD, contact Sound Word Associates, PO Box 2036, Chesterton, Indiana 46304. Request CD ia0536.

[23]Kirk and Kutchins, http://www.academyanalyticarts.org/kirk&kutchins.htm (Accessed 04/26/2015)

[24]Ibid

and Kutchins. "Although many of these attacks were on the validity of diagnosis, it was the reliability of diagnosis that became the focus of sustained attention among a few research psychiatrists," they state. "On the surface, diagnostic reliability seemed like the problem that needed to be resolved first, because the reliability of a classification scheme set a limit on its potential validity. If diagnoses could not be made consistently, little progress could be made on questions of empirical validity. Furthermore, reliability as a problem seemed easier to understand and appeared, at the time, to be a relatively easy problem to solve.

"Twenty years after the reliability problem became the central focus of DSM-III, there is still no single multi-site study showing that DSM (any version) is routinely used with high reliability by regular mental health clinicians. Nor is there credible evidence that any version of the manual has greatly increased its reliability beyond the previous version.

"If, as the developers of DSM-III insisted, an unreliable diagnostic system could not be valid, there is ample reason to conclude that the latest versions of DSM as a clinical tool are unreliable and therefore of questionable validity as a classification system. If the interpretations of the data regarding this critical, core problem have been somewhat misleading, how much confidence should we have in the hundreds of other changes in DSM that have been and will be justified by claims that they are based on science and data?"[25]

Despite doubts about the reliability of the DSM as a diagnostic tool, the DSM-IV was published in 1994 and the text revision (DSM-IV Revised) to that work was completed in 2000. The categories of mental disease or defect ballooned to 374.

The DSM-IV is "psychiatry's billing bible of 'disorders'" from which psychiatric screening, diagnoses, and their treatment are derived. Yet the disorders contained in the DSM-IV are arrived at by consensus, not by scientific criteria."There are no blood tests, brain scans, X-rays, MRIs (magnetic resonance imaging) or

---

[25] Ibid

'chemical imbalance' tests that can scientifically validate any mental 'disorder'as a disease or illness."[26]

Canadian psychologist Tana Dineen reports, "Unlike medical diagnoses that convey a probable cause, appropriate treatment and likely prognosis, the disorders listed in DSM-IV are terms arrived at through peer consensus—literally, a vote by APA committee members."[27]

CCEF's Dr. Michael R. Emlet, says, "It's important to remember that psychiatric diagnoses are descriptions of a struggling person's thoughts, emotions, and behaviors; they are not explanations for them. They tell you what but not why. The DSM admits that. So what's the problem? What's wrong with giving a name to a set of symptoms? Isn't that generally how the diagnostic system has historically evolved?

The problem is this: giving a summary label to a set of symptoms gives the appearance of explanation, particularly in our medicalized culture. It suggests that each diagnosis is a discrete and largely brain-determined entity, and there is simply little evidence for that except in the major psychiatric categories of schizophrenia, bipolar disorder, and severe depression. Even in these entities, we must realize the complex interaction of multiple factors."[28]

This may help to explain the widespread increase in mental diagnoses across the country. According to The National Institute for Mental Health in 2010, nationwide over 57.7 million people were diagnosed with a mental disorder.[29]

Major Depressive Disorder is the number one leading cause of disability in the United States. The number one diagnosis is Major Depressive Disorder, which accounts for 14.8 million American adults, or about 6.7 percent of the U.S. population. Dysthymic disorder (chronic, mild depression) affects approximately 1.5 percent

[26]Ken Kramer and Sue Weibert, "Teen Screen: A Front Group for the Psycho-pharmaceutical Industrial Complex," Data Search Worldwide, Inc. Feb. 18, 2006, http://www.psycsearch.net/teenscreen.html PsychSearch.net is a public service informational project that makes government records available concerning psych abuses.

[27]Ibid

[28]Mike Emlet "DSM-5: The New Normal?" CCEF Blog May 22, 2013 http://www.ccef.org/blog/dsm-5-new-normal? (accessed March 17 2015)

[29]"From Discovery to Cure," August 2010 Report of the National Advisory Mental Health Council's Workgroup, pg. 1, accessed 3/17/2014 at http://www.nimh.nih.gov

of the U.S. population age 18 and older in a given year. This figure translates to about 3.3 million American adults. Approximately 40 million Americans have an anxiety disorder, 6 million have panic disorder, and 5.7 million American adults have been diagnosed with bi-polar disorder. (Source: U.S. Census Bureau Population Estimates by Demographic Characteristics. Table 2: Annual Estimates of the Population by Selected Age Groups and Sex for the United States: April 1, 2000 to July 1, 2004 (NC-EST2004-02) Source: Population Division, U.S. Census Bureau Release Date: June 9, 2005.) Over ten million children were diagnosed with ADD in 2010, an increase of 66 percent since the year 2000.[30]

In his lecture entitled, "Chemical Imbalances: Scientific Fact or Social Phenomenon," Dr. Kurt Grady addresses how a diagnosis is included in the DSM. He says, "These diagnoses and the others contained in the DSM are not related to laboratory testing and medical discoveries. Mental disorders are decided without any scientific study or procedure. They are included in the manual by the hand-votes of psychiatrists and psychologists, essentially sitting around a table discussing what they think is a disease in the same manner as they would decide where to go for dinner! In 2001, the DSM-IV was voted as one of the ten worst psychiatric publications of the millennium and called 'A monster out of control.'"[31]

Stuart Kirk, professor emeritus of social welfare at UCLA says, "The whole disease model that underlies the DSM has been an utter scientific failure…There's not a single biological marker for any of the 300-plus disorders. What we do instead is descriptive. This describing is creating a disorder and pretending it's a medical illness rather than just human behavior."[32]

---

[30]Katherine Bindley "ADHD diagnoses in children up 66 Percent" 3/21/2012 http://www.huffingtonpost.com/2012/03/21/adhd-diagnoses-up-by-66-perent_n_1370793.html (Accessed 3/17/2015)

[31]Op cit, Grady

[32]Sharon Jayson, USA Today, "Books blast new version of psychiatry's bible, the DSM," 05/12/2013 http://www.usatoday.com/story/news/nation/2013/05/12/dsm-psychiatry-mental-disorders/2150819/ (Accessed 04/26/2015)

Thomas Insel, director of the National Institute of Mental Health, said the DSM is "at best, a dictionary, creating a set of labels and defining each" and that "its weakness is its lack of validity." He says NIMH will reorient its research away from the manual because "DSM diagnoses are based on a consensus about clusters of clinical symptoms, not any objective laboratory measure."[33]

The new DSM-5 was reported to have had major problems prior to publication. The APA has published numerous articles addressing the compromising of psychiatric diagnosis by the use of "abysmal results" in the field trials. "The results of the DSM 5 field trials are a disgrace to the field."[34]

Another article states the DSM is "in distress" and that the DSM 5 Task Force was willing to accept poor quality in field trial results to move forward with publication.[35]

According to Allen Frances, the chairman of the DSM-IV task force: "DSM-5 has never had anyone on board who could write a clean, consistent, unambiguous criteria set. DSM-5 appears to have received either no editing at all, or amateur editing at best. Getting the words right is certainly not enough, but if you can't even get them right, nothing else can ever be safe."[36]

"The DSM-5, the recently published fifth edition of the diagnostic manual, ignored this risk and introduced several high-prevalence diagnoses at the fuzzy boundary with normality."

For example, the DSM-5 opens the door for patients worried about having a medical illness to be diagnosed with somatic symptom disorder. Normal grief may be misdiagnosed as major depressive disorder, and the forgetfulness of old age may now be interpreted as mild neurocognitive disorder.

---

[33] op cit, Jayson

[34] Frances, Allen J., MD "Newsflash From APA Meeting: DSM 5 Has Flunked Its Reliability Tests" Psychology Today, 05/26/2012 http://www.psychologytoday.com/blog/dsm5-in-distress/201205/newsflash-apa-meeting-dsm-5-has-flunked-its-reliability-tests accessed 03/17/2015

[35] Frances, Allen J., MD "DSM 5: How Reliable is Reliable Enough? http://www.psychologytoday.com/blog/dsm5-in-distress/201201/dsm-5-how-reliable-is-reliable-enough 01/18/2012, accessed 03/17/2015

[36] Op Cit Frances, "Newsflash From APA Meeting: DSM 5 Has Flunked its Reliability Tests" accessed 03/17/2015

"The already overused diagnosis of attention-deficit disorder will be even easier to apply to adults thanks to criteria that have been loosened further," Dr. Frances adds. Other changes in the DSM-5 will allow clinicians to label a child with temper tantrums as having disruptive mood dysregulation disorder, and overeating can now be called binge eating disorder.

The real danger in diagnostic inflation is over diagnosis and overtreatment of patients who are essentially well, he says. "Drug companies take marketing advantage of the loose DSM definitions by promoting the misleading idea that everyday life problems are actually undiagnosed psychiatric illness caused by a chemical imbalance and requiring a solution in pill form. New psychiatric diagnoses are now potentially more dangerous than new psychiatric drugs," Dr. Frances advises.[37]

We are in the midst of a virtual epidemic brought about by the mental health profession, which should be of great concern to our society! Our schools, hospitals, nuclear power plants, and churches are full of people who have been diagnosed with some sort of mental illness including depression. These individuals have been prescribed medication without any objective medical testing to prove that a disease is present. Think about this: people in whose hands we routinely place our lives—your airplane pilot, medical doctor, surgeon, teacher, police personnel, and government offcials—may have been diagnosed with a mental illness and may be taking one or more antidepressants or other psychotropic medication.

Selling Sickness

"The way to sell drugs is to sell psychiatric illness."—Carl Elliot, a bioethicist from the University of Minnesota, quoted in "Drug Ads Hyping Anxiety Make Some Uneasy," Washington Post, July 16, 2001, page A01.

The U.S. Centers for Disease Control and Prevention (CDC) recently reported that antidepressant use in the United States has increased nearly 400 percent in the last two decades, making antide-

---

[37]Harrison, Pam, "Use DSM-5 'Cautiously, If at All,' DSM-IV Chair Advises" Medscape Medical News, 05/17/2013http://www.medscape.com/viewarticle/804378 accessed 11/23/2015

pressants the most frequently used class of medications by Americans ages 18-44. Among Americans 12 years and older, 11 percent were taking antidepressants by 2005-2008 (the most recently reported study period), and 23 percent of women ages 40-59 years were taking them.[38]

According to scientists at Harvard University and the University of Michigan, the cost of depression to the economy, including increased medical expenses, is estimated to be 83 billion dollars per year. Depressed people lose 5.6 hours of productive work every week when they are depressed, according to the Journal of the American Medical Association.[39]

Eighty percent of depressed people are impaired in their daily functioning, according to the Centers for Disease Control and Prevention (CDC).[40] Fifty percent of the loss of work productivity is due to absenteeism and short-term disability. In any 30 day period, depressed workers have 1.5 to 3.2 more short-term disability days, according to the American Psychiatric Association.[41]

"In today's society, many believe that most abhorrent behavior can be corrected by the right combination of medications that target the faulty set of neurotransmitters in the brain," says Kurt Grady, of the IABC. He adds that the average hospital stay for a person with mental illness is 7.1 days. "Biopsychiatry is big business," Grady explains.[42]

The use of psychotropic drugs by adult Americans increased 22 percent from 2001 to 2010, with one in five adults now taking

[38]Levine, Bruce: 400% Rise in Anti-Depressant Pill Use: Americans Are Disempowered -- Can the OWS Uprising Shake Us Out of Our Depression? From Alternet, http://www.alternet.org/story/152873/400_rise_in_anti-depressant_pill_use%3A_americans_are_disempowered_--_can_the_ows_uprising_shake_us_out_of_our_depression (Accessed 11/27/2015)

[39]Leahy, Robert Ph.D., "The Cost of Depression" Huffington Post Blog 10/30/2010, http://www.huffingtonpost.com/robert-leahy-phd/the-cost-of-depression_b_770805.html (Accessed 03/17/2015)

[40]CDC Publications and Information Products, NCHS Data Brief http://www.cdc.gov/nchs/data/databriefs/db07.htm Accessed 03/17/2015

[41]Locklear, Michael, "Depression costs America As Much As The War In Afghanistan" Self-Growth.com, Mental Health http://voices.yahoo.com/depression-costs-america-as-much-as-war-afghanistan-8246661.html?cat=72 Accessed 03/17/2015

[42]Op Cit, Grady

at least one psychotropic medication, according to industry data. In 2010, Americans spent more than $16 billion on antipsychotics, $11 billion on antidepressants and $7 billion for drugs to treat attention-deficit hyperactivity disorder (ADHD). The rapid growth of all three classes of drugs has alarmed some mental health professionals, who are concerned about the use of powerful antipsychotic drugs by elderly nursing home residents, and the prescription of stimulants to children who may have been misdiagnosed with ADHD.[43]

Antidepressant use has also skyrocketed because of the increased practice of prescribing antidepressants for many conditions other than severe depression, and prescribing them for longer periods of time. Among the 2005-2008 antidepressant user group (no data offered on earlier study periods), only 33.9 percent had severe symptoms of depression; 28.4 percent of antidepressant users had moderate symptoms; and 19.2 percent had mild symptoms; while 7.6 percent had no depression symptoms. And, according to the CDC report, more than 60 percent of Americans who are taking antidepressants have taken them for 2 years or longer, with 14 percent having taken them for 10 years or more.

Grady says that "armies of highly motivated and well-trained pharmaceutical representatives visit doctors' offices seven days a week promoting medications and leaving samples. The phy-sicians are recruited by the pharmaceutical companies as advisors and they pay them to give their opinion on the most recent advertis-ing campaign."[44]

An unholy alliance exists between the pharmaceutical companies, science, and the mental health industry. This results in drugs for everything from adjustment disorder to workaholism. One consequence of all this medical intervention has been a removal of responsibility for behavior and an inability or refusal to deal with the real issues plaguing an individual. The DSM-5 contains redefinitions of sub-categories of disorders and illnesses that will make every person eligible for some diagnosis of mental illness.

[43]Smith, Brendan L, "Inappropriate Prescribing" American Psychological Association Monitor On Psychology http://www.apa.org/monitor/2012/06/prescribing.aspx Accessed 03/17/2015

[44]Op Cit, Grady

Many respected physicians, neuroscientists, psychiatrists, and psychologists have begun to expose this biopsychiatric pseudoscience for what it is—deception. According to the late Dr.Thomas Szasz, professor of psychiatry emeritus at the State University of New York, Health Science Center, and author of more than 30 books exposing and questioning the legitimacy of his field, "The primary function and goal of the DSM is to lend credibility to the claim that certain behaviors or, more correctly, misbehaviors are mental disorders and that such disorders are, therefore, medical diseases.

"Thus, pathological gambling enjoys the same status as myocardial infarction (blood clot in heart artery). In effect, the APA maintains that betting is something the patient cannot control, and that generally all psychiatric 'symptoms' or 'disorders' are outside the patient's control. I reject that claim as patently false. The ostensible validity of the DSM is reinforced by psychiatry's claim that mental illnesses are brain diseases—a claim supposedly based on recent discoveries in neuroscience, made possible by imaging techniques for diagnosis and pharmacological agents for treatment. That claim is not true. There are no objective diagnostic tests to confirm or disconfirm the diagnosis of depression; the diagnosis can and must be made solely on the basis of the patient's appearance and behavior and the reports of others about his or her behavior.

"There is no blood or other biological test to ascertain the presence or absence of a mental illness, as there is for most bodily diseases. If such a test were developed, then the condition would cease to be a mental illness and would be classified as a symptom of a bodily disease."[45]

The question begs to be asked: What causes depression?

Depression as an Illness

Read the following case examples:

Case #1

One morning you wake up and start experiencing nausea and

[45]CCHR International, "Professor Thomas Szasz On The Diagnostic and Statistical Manual of Mental Disorders," http://www.cchrint.org/about-us/co-founder-dr-thomas-szasz/quotes-on-dsm/ accessed 03/17/2015

the feeling of pressure in your chest. You have pain in your arm; your chest feels heavy. You take antacids and medication for indigestion for a few days, but it doesn't seem to be getting any better.

You begin to think that maybe there is something more going on here than a little indigestion. You go to the doctor and tell him that you have been feeling nauseous with pressure in your chest and pain in your arm over the last several days . The doctor asks you to describe what else you might have been feeling and what you have been doing to relieve your symptoms.

The doctor runs some tests. You have an EKG, blood work, and chest x-ray, and before you leave the offce, you are told you must have immediate open heart surgery. You are, of course, quite surprised at this—he may not have received many, if any, test results back yet, and he wants to cut your chest open! You ask your doctor why he wants to do open heart surgery. He tells you that you have reported to him all the signs and symptoms of a person having heart disease and maybe even a heart attack!

You ask him about your test results. He tells you the EKG is normal, the blood work is normal, and the x-ray is normal. Why then, you ask the doctor, does he want to do surgery on one of the most vital organs in your body?

He tells you that you have described to him the signs and symptoms of someone with heart disease or a heart attack. But, you reply, all your tests are normal! The doctor tells you that it doesn't matter; you have described the symptoms of a person who has heart disease, and he wants to make your symptoms go away. Your symptom reporting is what leads to the diagnosis and the treatment.

Case #2

A woman feels tired and listless and has little appetite. She feels sad and has been crying and sleeping a lot for the last few days or weeks, so she goes to the doctor. She reports these symptoms to the doctor. The doctor asks how long these symptoms have persisted, takes blood for a lab work–up, and sends her out the door with samples and a prescription for Prozac.

176

Case #3

A woman has been suffering with recurrent migraine head-aches and is questioning the cause. She once had Lyme disease and also has had trouble with pain in her neck, back, and shoulders for the past several years. She has been on Imitrex and other medications as needed for the pain, but they don't seem to help. She asks about an MRI because she is concerned about a brain tumor. The physician tells her she is depressed because of the pain and offers her samples of Zoloft and a prescription.

The first case is a dramatization, but the others are true. In each of the real cases, a patient went to a medical professional for answers and was sent on her way with samples and a prescription for a pill to alter the chemistry of one of the most vital organs in her body–her brain. In all cases where blood work is done, it will come back normal, unless the person has a biological illness such as diabetes, a thyroid condition, an infection, some form of cancer, or another organic disease.

How many times have you gone to the doctor feeling just terrible, with aches, congestion, sore throat, and bad cough? You go because you want something to make you feel better. You want an antibiotic because you are sure you have some infection. The doctor runs blood tests that come back normal. What does the doctor tell you? "Sorry, blood work is normal, with no detectable signs of disease that would need medication. You will feel better in a few days, but it could take up to two weeks."

The doctor is unwilling to give you an antibiotic that you don't need because he can't medically prove you need it. Your symptoms and complaints do not warrant his risking your overall health by giving you a medication that won't treat the real problem. That would be bad medicine.

You cannot have an antibiotic, but you can have an antidepressant— even though he cannot medically prove you need it.

How is Depression Diagnosed?

In this section, we will look at some psychological "evidence" for the cause of depression and such depression-related conditions as "mental illness".

Diagnosis of depression is based on behavior, not on changes in the body. In most cases, depression should not be called an illness at all. What may surprise you is that all of the testing for depression is subjective, not objective. The diagnosis of depression is made from an evaluation of the person's feelings, thinking, and behavior.[46]

Some of the behaviors and symptoms the depressed person may manifest are:
- A depressed mood for most of the day, occurring most days in a two-week period
- Unexplained sadness
- Decreased interest in and little pleasure from daily activities
- Increased or decreased appetite which results in weight loss or gain
- Difficulty sleeping or excessive sleeping
- Psychomotor agitation (repetitive behavior that is unproduc-tive: pacing, wringing of hands, etc.) or psychomotor retardation (slowed-down behaviors)
- Feelings of worthlessness
- Preoccupation with guilt
- Diminished capacity to think and concentrate
- Recurrent thoughts of death
- Difficulty at work or school, at home, and in social situations(due to depression)
- Various physical ailments or hypochondriac tendencies
- Lethargy
- Loss of relationships
- Irrational irritability
- Loss of interest in spiritual activities
- Loss of confidence in God and His love
- Exaggerated emotions
- Self-pitying speech
- Tendency to blame people or circumstances for faults or problems
- Blames self, declares self as hopeless, entirely at fault.

---

[46] Asher, Marshal and Mary, *The Christian's Guide to Psychological Terms*, Bermidij, MN: Focus Pulishing, 2004, pg

Biological Disease Diagnosis

What you may not know is that in order for an illness to be considered a true illness, science requires objective, measurable, reproducible testing, according to Dan Wickert, M.D., an obstetrician, gynecologist and ACBC certified counselor. "To qualify as an illness, the problem must involve tissue damage and be demonstrated by abnormal function. The diagnosis must be a provable, knowable fact based on objective testing," he says. "In medicine, an illness has a definite organic cause."[47]

Mental Illness Diagnosis

Currently, no objective, measurable, reproducible tests exist to prove scientifically that depression is an illness, says Dr. Robert Smith, author of The Christian Counselor's Medical Desk Reference.[48]

In 1992, a panel of experts assembled by the U.S. Congress Office of Technology Assessment concluded: "Many questions remain about the biology of mental disorders. In fact, research has yet to identify specific biological causes for any of these disorders . . . Mental disorders are classified on the basis of symptoms because there are no biological markers or laboratory tests for them."[49] Au-thor and psychiatrist Peter Breggin says, "There is no evidence that any of the common psychological or psychiatric disorders have a genetic or biological component."[50]

Look again at the list of symptoms for depression and you will see that the criteria for the diagnosis of depression is based on subjective reasoning and thinking—not on changes in the body. Other so-called mental illnesses are diagnosed in the same manner.

---

[47] Wickert, Dan, Depression, audio CD of lecture presented at Faith Baptist Biblical Counseling Training Conference, Lafayette, Indiana (Feb 8, 2001)

[48] Smith, Robert D., The Christian Counselor's Medical Desk Reference, Stanley, NC: Timeless Tests, 200, pg. 198

[49] The Biology of Mental Disorders, (U.S. Government Printing Office, 1992), 13-14, 46-47. As Quoted by Lawrence Stevens, J.D., "Does Mental Illness Exist?" http://www.antipsychiatry.org/exist.htm (Accessed 04/26/2015)

[50] Breggin, Peter Toxic Psychiatry, New York: St. Martin's Press, 1991, pg. 291

The patient usually goes to the doctor with one or more of the symptoms listed above, and the physician or clinician uses a screening tool to determine which and how many of the criteria in the DSM-5 the client meets.

The professional, using an interview questionnaire such as the Beck Depression Inventory, asks the patient 21 multiple-choice questions and "attempts to assess a specific symptom or attitude 'which appear(s) to be specific to depressed patients, and which are consistent with descriptions of the depression contained in the psychiatric literature.'"[51]

The questions are based mostly on how the client feels. For example, does the person feel sad, discouraged, dissatisfied, better, or worse than anyone else? The Internet gives access to hundreds of websites created by pharmaceutical companies that each have their own depression screening tool. The individual can identify the common symptoms of depression by completing an online questionnaire and taking it to a "professional" for a complete diagnosis. The so-called professional then repeats the same assessment in similar fashion and hopefully performs some medical testing to rule out a medical condition.

Physically Induced (Biological) Depression

There are legitimate and provable medical causes for feeling depressed. Before admitting a patient to a psychiatric ward in a hospital, the attending physician must determine that the symptoms the patient is demonstrating are not the result of an undiagnosed medical condition. Various medical tests are performed, such as EKG (electrocardiogram), X-ray, and blood and urine analysis. The patient is admitted to the psychiatric ward of the hospital only when all medical tests prove the symptoms are not due to a medical condition (non-organic) or when there is a medical condition (organic in nature) that needs to be stabilized and is contributing to depression. When a counselee tells me that he or she has felt depressed for an extended period of time, the first instruction I give is to get a medi-

---

[51]Beck Depression Inventory (BDI), The Psychological Corporation, nova.edu/~cpphelp/BDI.html (Accessed 04/26/2015)

cal exam. In the biological realm, more than 70 diseases can lead to physically induced depression, with chronic illness being a chief contributor. A chronic illness is one that tends to last a long time or one that cannot be cured. "Depression can 'co-occur' or be triggered by an existing medical condition. The physical effects of depression are very real and often debilitating, but only around 10-18 percent of depression is triggered by another medical condition."[52]

Which Long-Term Illnesses Can Lead to Depression?

Up to one-third of those with a serious illness experience symptoms of depression. In fact, depression is one of the most common complications of chronic illness. The physical changes that occur as a result of the illness can trigger depression. The remedy for this type of depression is to treat or eliminate the physical cause, if possible. The counselee may have to learn how to adjust to the demands of the illness or the treatments for the illness. Some illnesses will drastically alter the life of the counselee, which can bring profound sadness, anger, and loss of hope.[53]

Examples of chronic illnesses include:

- Heart attack: 40-65 percent experience depression
- Coronary artery disease (without heart attack): 18-20 percent experience depression
- Parkinson's disease: 40 percent experience depression
- Multiple sclerosis: 40 percent experience depression
- Stroke: 10-27 percent experience depression
- Cancer: 25 percent experience depression
- Diabetes: 25 percent experience depression[54]

[52]"Medical Causes of Depression" Depression Learning path, http://www.clinical-depression.co.uk/sites/clinical-depression.co.uk/files/Depression-Learning-Path-Free.pdf (Accessed 04/26/2015)

[53]"Chronic Illness," Health Information Center, Diseases and Conditions, The Cleveland Clinic Foundation http://my.clevelandclinic.org/health/diseases_conditions/hic_Coping_With_Chronic_Illnesses accessed 03/18/2015

[54]WebMD, Depression Health Center: "Dealing with Chronic Illnesses and Depression" http://www.webmd.com/depression/guide/chronic-illnesses-depression#1 Accessed 03/18/2015

Less than 5 percent of depression cases are physically induced and do not respond to counseling, according to Dr. Bill Gillham, cofounder of Lifetime Guarantee Ministries. Conditions such as "PMS, hypoglycemia, diabetes, hormonal imbalance, thyroid or blood sugar problems, etc., are physical factors which can cause depression."[55]

When one has an organic problem or a diseased organ, every medical treatment may be attempted and the organ that is diseased will not change. You cannot make a diseased pancreas healthy; you cannot make a thyroid function. The best that can be done is to medicate the body to simulate what the diseased organ can no longer do or replace the organ.

In cases of organic or biologic illness, scientific proof can support the fact that the body is not working properly. Many times, what brings the patient to the office is that he or she is not feeling right, is not feeling well, or is even feeling depressed. The doctor then runs blood tests and organ function tests to determine if a medi-cal reason exists for why the patient does not feel well. If the tests come back with a result that deviates from what is known to be scientifically normal, the patient is diagnosed with a disease. This explains medically why the patient has been feeling poorly.

Non-Organic (Reactive) Depression

A reactive depression is different from a biological depres-sion. There is no medical testing to support this diagnosis. It is a short-term response to a stressful or painful life. Its psychological term is Adjustment Disorder. This type of depression is an excessive response to something traumatic in life, such as the loss of a job or a breakup of a relationship. Like all the diagnoses for non-organic depression, the diagnosis is based on subjectivity and symptoms re-ported by the patient.

---

[55]"Free From Depression," Discipleship Journal, Lifetime Ministries, http://www.life-time.org/?s=Depression (Accessed 04/26/2015)

The Chemical Imbalance Theory

It is important to understand that any health concern or disease can alter the processes of the human body and produce a chemical imbalance. These imbalances are usually detected by blood or urine analysis. For example, when a chemical imbalance is identified in the thyroid, the diagnosis is typically hypothyroidism or hyperthyroidism. If a chemical imbalance is identified in the pancreas, it is usually called diabetes. It is no longer classified or diagnosed as a chemical imbalance. Rather, it is given the correct medical term, and effective treatment is begun that will correct the imbalance in the body.

Outside of a biological problem, "chemical imbalance" is the term used for the theory that one of the chemicals (neurotransmitters) in the synaptic junction of the brain is abnormal (too high or too low). The simple diagram below will help us understand what we know about the brain and the chemicals in the brain.

When passing a message in the brain to convey happiness, for example, a sending nerve cell sends information via an electrical impulse that triggers the release of chemical neurotransmitters like serotonin, norepinephrine, and dopamine to a receiving nerve cell. This process ensures that messages move forward and that nerve cells continue to communicate.

Neurotransmitters move across the synapse

Sending Nerve Ending--- → |synapse/gap (measured in nanometers)|--- →Receiving Nerve Ending

The synapse contains several hundred types of neurotransmitting chemicals. These are the ones referenced most frequently:

- Catecholamine (cat-e-KOHL-o-mine)
- Norepinephrine
- Dopamine
- Serotonin
- Epinephrine

The Chemical Imbalance theory says that because these chemicals are "abnormal", they interfere with the transfer of impulses from nerve endings in the synaptic junction, which results in bad feelings and behavior. To determine what an abnormal level of these chemicals is, we must first know what normal is. It is impossible, however, to know what normal is for any brain chemical at this time. Medical science has not advanced to the point where it can determine a normal level of brain chemical. The synaptic junction is so tiny that it cannot be measured, nor can scientists measure the amount of each of the hundreds of chemicals in that junction.

Since the original publication of this book, the theory of chemical imbalance is no longer widely accepted as medical fact among mainstream medical professionals and researchers. More and more of them are finally agreeing with what Szasz, Glenmullen, and Breggin have been saying from the beginning: There is a complete lack of medical evidence to prove the chemical imbalance theory. "Further, even today we do not know what the correct balance of serotonin, dopamine, or norepinephrine should be in the human brain."[56] Despite this, some continue to promote this theory and the drugs that are supposed to treat it. [57]

One excellent article I read asked the question: "'How well supported is the Chemical Imbalance Theory in the current scientific research?' The answer to this question was shocking, but consistent: "Not at all!"[58] In book after book, article after article, over the past five or so years that I've been studying this topic, I have not encountered one shred of solid evidence for this theory. In fact, the only places I could find support for the theory were on commercial websites and advertisements promoting antidepressants and other psychiatric drugs. Given the prevalence of this theory, I was stunned to find how many researchers, doctors, psychiatrists, inves-

[56]Hodges, Charles: *Good Mood, Bad Mood* Shepherd press Wapwallopen, Pennsylvania

[57]Lacasse, Jeffrey R. and Leo, Jonathan: Serotonin and Depression: A Disconnect Between the Advertisements and the Scientific Literature http://journals.plos.org/plosmedicine/article?id=10.1371/journal.pmed.0020392 accessed 03/18/2015

[58]Morning Light Counseling Library, "Chemical Imbalance: What the Research Says" http://counselinglibrary.org/healing/depression/chemical-imbalance (Accessed 04/26/2015)

tigative journalists, scientists, counselors, and other professionals have come out publicly declaring their opposition to it.

Dr. Joseph Glenmullen, author of Prozac Backlash, says, "In medicine, strict criteria exist for calling a condition a disease. In addition to a predictable cluster of symptoms, the cause of the symptoms or some understanding of their physiology must be established...We do not yet have proof either of the cause or the physiology for any psychiatric diagnosis...In recent decades, we have had no shortage of alleged biochemical imbalances for psychiatric conditions. Diligent though these attempts have been, not one has been proven. Quite the contrary. In every incidence where such an imbalance was thought to have been found, it was later proven false."[59]

Contemporary neuroscience research has failed to confirm any serotonergic lesion in any mental disorder, and has in fact provided significant counterevidence to the explanation of a simple neurotransmitter deficiency. Modern neuroscience has instead shown that the brain is vastly complex and poorly understood.[60]

Expert after expert is now coming forward to state that the chemical imbalance theory lacks any scientific evidence to prove it exists. This is what some noted experts conclude about the theory of chemical imbalance:

In 1996, psychiatrist David Kaiser said, "Modern psychiatry has yet to convincingly prove the genetic/biologic cause of any single mental illness. . . Patients [have] been diagnosed with 'chemical imbalances' despite the fact that no test exists to support such a claim, and . . . there is no real conception of what a correct chemical balance would look like."[61]

Elliot Valenstein, Ph.D., author of Blaming the Brain, is unequivocal: "[T]here are no tests available for assessing the chemical status of a living person's brain." No "biochemical, anatomical, or

---

[59] op.cit Glenmullen, 192-193

[60] Horgan, John, *The Undiscovered Mind* Simon and Schuster/Touchstone, New York, New York, 1999

[61] Kaiser, David: "Commentary: Against Biologic Psychiatry, Psychiatric Times, vol. 13, issue 12 (December 1996) http://www.psychiatrictimes.com/articles/commentary-against-biologic-psychiatry (Accessed 03/22/2015)

functional signs have been found that reliably distinguish the brains of mental patients."[62]

Valenstein is not alone. "In an explosive admission, American Psychiatric Association president Steven Sharfstein did a 180-degree turn-around from his TODAY Show interview (June 27, 2005) and admitted that there is no way to test for a 'chemical imbalance' as the cause for mental disorders. People magazine (July 11) quoted Dr. Sharfstein conceding, 'We do not have a clean-cut lab test.'"[63]

Neurologist Fred Baughman exposes the absence of bona fide diseases in psychiatry, quoting Dutch psychiatrist Hermann van Praag, who says that researchers thought they had discovered a deficiency in a chemical cousin to serotonin in the cerebrospinal fluid of some depressed patients. "In the end, the deficiency proved neither diagnostic nor specific for any psychiatric condition."[64] Nevertheless, patients are given the impression that a definitive serotonin deficiency in depression is firmly established when none has been found.

While there has been no shortage of biochemical explanations for psychiatric conditions, Glenmullen is emphatic: "Not one (disease, chemical imbalance) has been proven. In every instance where such an imbalance was thought to have been found, it was later proven false."[65]

Currently, the existence of a chemical imbalance cannot be supported or proven through medical testing or blood testing. The only way a person can be accurately tested for some of these brain disorders is by taking a brain sample—a biopsy of the brain—which is not recommended for living people. Chemical imbalance theories are simply guesses; theories that cannot be tested by any other method than by subjective data accumulation.

---

[62]Valenstein, Elliot: *Blaming the Brain* (New York: The Free Press, 1998), p 4

[63]PR Web: http://www.prweb.com/releases/2005/07/prweb257630.htm Accessed 03/23/2015

[64]Fred A. Baughman, Jr., "Neurology and Child Neurology," Oikos, www.oikos.org\ neurology&childneurology.htm quoting Herman M. Van Praag, "Make-Believes" in Psychiatry (Brunner-Routledge, 1993). (Accessed 04/26/2015)

[65] op.cit Glenmullen, 198

Brain Scans

The methods currently in vogue for diagnosing depression and other so-called mental illnesses are the use of the PET scan (positron emission topography), which visualizes regional energy utilization in the brain and a SPECT (Single Photon Emission Computed Tomography), which visualizes functional information about a patient's specific organ or body system.

"Brain imaging techniques are currently the favorite tool used by biopsychiatrists to argue for a purported physiological cause for the various phenomena called 'mental illnesses,' largely because the scans yield brightly colored pictures of the brain—almost like coloring book drawings—which can be shown to the public and which appear to offer highly dramatic demonstrations of something 'wrong' with the brain that has fewer bright colors in it. The public generally knows little about either scientific method or logical inference, and even less about the interpretation of brain scans, and so is likely to be mightily impressed by this 'scientific evidence.'"[66]

"Perhaps because the criteria for categorizing the subjects are so nebulous as to be nearly arbitrary might be a good place to begin. Or should one discuss the fact that everything from play-ing music to asking the subject to think about a particular thing will radically alter PET and SPECT images of the brain? The idea that brain imaging studies prove that the wildly divergent phenomena that are grouped under the label 'mental illness' are brain diseases doesn't need to be torn to shreds: it is essentially nonsensical in the first place."[67]

Others agree that claims of using brain scans to make psychiatric diagnosis are not valid. Psychiatrist M. Douglas Mar says, "There is no scientific basis for these claims. At minimum, patients should be told that SPECT is highly controversial.[68]

[66]Eaton T. Forest, "There are no 'Chemical Imbalances,'" Eaton T. Forest Research Center, 2003, http://www.academyanalyticarts.org/fores.htm (Accessed 04/26/2015)

[67]Ibid

[68]Lisa M. Krieger, "Some Question Value of Brain Scan; Untested Tool Belongs in Lab Only, Experts Say" The Mercury News (May 2004)

The usual sleight of hand involves comparing photographs of a brain scan of a depressed patient and a non-depressed patient, where there happen to be other differences between the two brains. Sometimes the differences simply reflect normal variation and sometimes they reflect drug damage. Brain scans cannot show differences between the brains of depressed and normal patients because no such differences have been demonstrated."[69] Remember, just because various "experts" proclaim their theories as fact does not make them factual. You may have even heard Christian psychologists claim that brain scans can be used to make psychiatric diagnoses. The fact remains that chemical imbalance is a theory. Unfortunately, even some Christians will accept a theory that has no more proof than the theory of evolution.

If no reliable, reproducible medical tests are available to di-agnose depression or a chemical imbalance, we are left with only one frightening conclusion: A chemical imbalance deemed a mental illness is diagnosed based on the thoughts and feelings of the pa-tient. As discussed on previous pages, a person's thoughts, feelings and experiences do not set a standard for a medical illness.

It's important to remember that psychiatric diagnoses are descriptions of a struggling person's thoughts, emotions, and behaviors; they are not explanations for them. They tell you what but not why. The DSM admits that. So what's the problem? What's wrong with giving a name to a set of symptoms? Isn't that generally how the diagnostic system has historically evolved? The problem is this: Giving a summary label to a set of symptoms gives the appearance of explanation, particularly in our medicalized culture. It suggests that each diagnosis is a discrete and largely brain-determined en-tity, and there is simply little evidence for that except in the major psychiatric categories of schizophrenia, bipolar disorder, and severe

---

[69]Peter R. Breggin, *Reclaiming Our Children* (Cambridge, Massachusetts: Perseus Books, 200), 293

depression. Even in these entities, we must realize the complex interaction of multiple factors.[70]

This raises another question: If depression is not a true illness, then why do people feel better on medication? We live in a very feeling-oriented society. Many people cannot tolerate not feeling good, happy, successful, and accepted. When people are feeling miserable, sad, and depressed, their goal is to feel better. And 70-85 percent of people on psychotropic medications do feel better. When brain chemicals such as serotonin or dopamine are altered, they will cause a person to feel better.

Because feeling better helps the feeling-oriented person to function better, improved feeling and function are used as an argument to support the theory of chemical imbalance. The logic used is that if I felt bad before I took this medication, and now I feel better, there must have been something wrong with me that this medication has corrected.

How the medications improve the feelings of the person taking them is not known. Plenty of theories exist, but no proof. One theory is: The use of antidepressants as depression medication is based on artificially increasing the amount of neurotransmitters found in the synaptic cleft, the area between two synapses. Neurotransmitters act as communication agents between the synapses. When people are medicated, they may sense relief from guilt, sleep better; feel more energetic, and have a better outlook on life. This is the payoff they are searching for—the change from feeling bad to feeling good again

Typically, they can feel better for years, but eventually they may build up a tolerance to the level of medication, or may develop liver or other physical problems from extended use of the medication. Another little-known fact is that people have a 50- to 75-percent rate of recurrence of depression while taking medication. Because of this recurrence rate, researchers are continually developing new medications to replace the ones that do not work for every client.

---

[70]DSM-V: The New Normal? Mike Emlet, published May 22, 2013 at: http://www.ccef.org/blog/dsm-5-new-normal? (Accessed 5/22/13)

The Placebo Effect

More than half of the clinical trials sponsored by the pharmaceutical companies failed to find significant drug/placebo differences, and there were no advantages to higher doses of antidepressants. The small difference between antidepressant and placebo has been referred to as a "dirty little secret" by clinical trial researchers (Hollon et al., 2002, a secret that was believed by FDA officials to be "of no practical value to either the patient or prescriber."[71] "Fifty-seven percent of the trials funded by the pharmaceutical industry failed to show a significant difference between drug and placebo."[72] In January of 2008 the media was ablaze with reports about the fact that the makers of antidepressants like Prozac© and Paxil© never published the results of about a third of the drug trials that they con-ducted because the results showed that a placebo was as effective or more effective than their drugs!

In February of 2008, Fox News ran a story that said antidepressants may not work as well in people who are mildly depressed as they do in patients with major depression, according to a new study published in the journal Public Library of Science Medicine. Researchers from various U.S., U.K. and Canadian universities found that some patients taking antidepressants believe the drugs are working for them, but many times it is only a placebo effect. The research team based its findings on 47 clinical trials, using drugs such as fluoxetine (Prozac©)and paroxetine (Paxil©),which are selective serotonin re-uptake inhibitors (SSRIs), and venlafaxine (Effexor©), a serotonin-norepinephrine re-uptake inhibitor.[73]

Psychological Treatment Options for the Depressed Person

For the greater part of the last 40 years, an unbiblical theory on how to treat depressed persons has been promoted and preached.

---

[71]Leber, 1998, as cited in Kirsch et al., 2002, Psychiatric Times, Sept 2002.

[72]Kirsch, I., et al., "Response to the Commentaries: Antidepressants and Placebos: Secrets, Revelations, and Unanswered Questions," Prevention & Treatment, 5:33 (July 15, 2002), Accessed 04/26/2015 at http://www.baumhedlundlaw.com/24.pdf

[73]http://www.foxnews.com/story/0,2933,332617,00.html (Accessed 04/26/2015)

Society has accepted that only psychology can handle the deep issues of human problems. Mental health professionals have concluded that a person's feelings are at the core of his problems. These feelings are often diagnosed to be the result of deep psychological issues. In order to understand those feelings, the client is told that he must have professional help by one who is trained in psychology or another area of mental health. The patient often receives therapy in conjunction with medication to discuss the feelings associated with his illness and to assist the patient on the road to feeling normal again.

The common forms of treatment in the field of psychiatry and psychology include:

Psychotherapy, or Counseling

Psychotherapy, which can be conducted by such health professionals as psychiatrists, psychologists, social workers, or psychiatric nurses, is a "systematic treatment method in which, during regularly scheduled meetings, the psychiatrist and patient discuss troubling problems and feelings….Depending on the extent of the problem, treatment may take just a few sessions over one or two weeks, or many sessions over several years."[74]

There are "many forms of psychotherapy…. psychotherapies that help patients change behaviors or thought patterns, psychotherapies that help patients explore the effect of past relationships and experiences on present behaviors, psychotherapies that treat troubled couples or families together, and more treatments that are tailored to help solve other problems in specific ways."[75]

Electroconvulsive Therapy

Also known as electroshock therapy or ECT, this medical treatment consists of six to twelve treatments, usually given three times a week for a month or less. While the patient is under general

---

[74]Federation of Texas Psychiatry, About Psychiatry: Most Common Treatments http://www.txpsych.org/aboutpsychiatrytreatments.htm (Accessed March 25, 2015)

[75]Ibid

anesthesia, the patient's brain is stimulated using a brief controlled series of electrical pulses, which causes a temporary seizure within the brain.

Self-Help Therapy

This generally refers to groups or meetings facilitated by a layperson (non-professional) who has been trained to assist people by providing a forum for talk therapy and interpersonal relating. The facilitator may also be a former group member or "survivor". These groups are intended to assist people to deal with death, abuse, accidents, addiction, or medical diagnosis.

Animal-Assisted Therapy

Animals are incorporated into therapy with the intention of creating empathy and compassion in a person. Pet therapy is used in an individual or group setting.

Art Therapy

This therapy uses drawing, painting, and sculpting to try to help people to reconcile inner conflicts, release deeply repressed emotions, and foster self-awareness, as well as personal growth. Some mental health providers use art therapy as both a diagnostic tool and as a way to help treat disorders such as depression, abuse-related trauma, and schizophrenia.

Dance/Movement Therapy

The underlying premise to dance/movement therapy is that it can help a person integrate the emotional, physical, and cognitive facets of "self".

Music/Sound Therapy

This relatively unexplored type of therapy may be used in conjunction with other therapies and may involve contemplative music (to soothe agitation and alleviate sadness), executive music (to strengthen self-confidence, creative music (composed and played by patients), and other forms of music intended to help speed recovery.[76]

The list goes on and on of possible therapeutic methods to treat someone with a mental illness, including the dangerous "re-birthing therapy", in which the patient is wrapped tightly in a blan-ket to represent the inside of a mother's womb and has to fight to get free as if going through the birth canal. There are many theories about how to help people, but no agreement on which theory is best or right. The therapist is free to choose which one of the theories he will use to help a client with his problems and get solutions. Many methods are proposed to help reduce the pain of the past and the present without scientific proof that any of them really work.

The methodology of the professionals is to use a theory of personality to determine what is normal. Once normal has been established, it is then possible to determine what is abnormal or unhealthy. The goal is to get the person to change back to normal. The glaring question is, who decides what is normal? What objective standard is there for normal? This is dangerous ground we tread upon.

If you choose to follow the path of professional counseling, I would encourage you to be wise and careful in your choices. As much effort as it may take for you to research the methods suggested by your caregiver, I would implore you to do so before beginning any kind of therapy.

As a suggestion, I have included some helps for you if you or someone you care about has sought or is going to seek medical or psychological help for depression. Here are some questions you might ask the treatment specialist:

---

[76] Aviansh De Sousa, "Music Therapy for Treatment of Psychiatric Disorders" Healthy Place/Alternative Mental Health Community, July 2014 http://www.healthyplace.com/ alternative-mental-health/treatments/music-therapy-for-treatment-of-psychiatric-disorders/ Accessed 03/26/2015

- What tests were run to prove a physical problem is present?
- How do those tests prove the presence of that physical problem?
- Is the condition a proven, demonstrable fact, or simply a theory?
- How do you know the alleged physical condition is the cause of the emotional or behavioral actions?
- Is the link a proven, demonstrable fact, or simply a theory?
- What proof do you have that the medicine you are recommending corrects the physical problem?

Friend, through biblical counseling, we have successfully helped many individuals identify what caused their depression or "mental illness", and through the use of the Scriptures and the hard work of life change through the power of the Holy Spirit they have gone on to live healthy, joyful (happy) normal lives. I pray this book has been a help to you in beginning to discover the root of your feelings of depression. I also hope that you have received enough information to cause you to pause before you take that giant leap into the world of psychopharmacology and treatment for something called a mental illness. May God bless you.

About the Author

Julie Ganschow is the founder of Reigning Grace Counseling Center in Kansas City Missouri. She earned a M.A. in Biblical Counseling and is certified as a Biblical Counselor with numerous organizations including the ACBC. She is a frequent conference and retreat speaker as well as teaching at a local Bible College. She is the author of *The Process of Biblical Change*, and *Living Beyond the Heart of Betrayal* in addition to writing for her daily blog at Biblical Counseling for Women (bc4women.org).
You can contact her at: reigninggracecounsel@rgcconline.org
Website: www.rgcconline.org

Printed in Great Britain
by Amazon

41942913R00109